The Intersection of Fashion and Disability

The Intersection of Fashion and Disability: A Historical Analysis

Kate Annett-Hitchcock

BLOOMSBURY VISUAL ARTS
LONDON • NEW YORK • OXFORD • NEW DELHI • SYDNEY

BLOOMSBURY VISUAL ARTS
Bloomsbury Publishing Plc
50 Bedford Square, London, WC1B 3DP, UK
1385 Broadway, New York, NY 10018, USA
29 Earlsfort Terrace, Dublin 2, Ireland

BLOOMSBURY, BLOOMSBURY VISUAL ARTS and the Diana logo are trademarks
of Bloomsbury Publishing Plc

First published in Great Britain in 2024

For legal purposes the Acknowledgements on p. xvi constitute an extension
of this copyright page.

Cover design: Eleanor Rose
Cover image © Vince Cavataio/Getty Images

A catalogue record for this book is available from the British Library.

A catalog record for this book is available from the Library of Congress.

ISBN: PB: 978-1-3501-4311-1
       HB: 978-1-3501-4310-4
       ePDF: 978-1-3501-4312-8
       eBook: 978-1-3501-4313-5

Typeset by RefineCatch Limited, Bungay, Suffolk
Printed and bound in India

To find out more about our authors and books visit www.bloomsbury.com
and sign up for our newsletters.

This book is dedicated to everyone who has ever felt marginalized by the fashion industry and those who wish to see change.

Contents

Illustrations

Foreword

Fashion continues to have an influence on certain disability objects. From Cutler and Gross's stance as the *'enfants terribles* of optometry', to Alleles' vision of 'fashion-forward' prosthetic covers, pioneering designers of eyewear and prosthetics have harnessed the culture and sensibilities of fashion design. Yet there seems less attention, and less revolution, when it comes to clothing itself. Clothing for disabled people and clothing for disabled-and-non-disabled people seems to have been less documented and discussed. And this is what this book is part of redressing.

Kate Annett-Hitchcock acknowledges her debt to other researchers and invites others to join this endeavour. Through its readability this book should also be an important bridge between academic scholarship and other cultural channels, from magazines to blogs and podcasts in which the reflections are no less deep and the influences may be wider still. Research, investigative journalism and activism need to be more entwined – as they are in the work of Liz Jackson, founder of The Disabled List, for example.

The Intersection of Fashion and Disability challenges what can be a simplistic and polarised framing of the relationship between disability and fashion. Applying labels to disabled people (rather than badges that they wear themselves, in Tom Shakespeare's distinction) reduces them; so too can fashion designers be reduced to stereotypes. I recall a conversation with a research team who were inclusively designing with a particular group of disabled wearers – yet had deliberately not involved any fashion designers. It was anathema to them to conceive the clothing as fashion, since then, they argued, it would go out of fashion. I really don't know what is worse: that fashion be deemed irrelevant to disabled people (and vice versa); or that anyone designing clothing might take such a simplistic view of what fashion is or represents; or even that deep pattern-cutting skills around fit and drape were not seen as contributing to the ways people might feel wearing these clothes.

This book corrects these oversimplifications through argument and example: among the most compelling of which is the designer Helen Cookman, whose contribution as an established fashion designer at Clothing Research, Inc. is documented in detail. The quotations of her own words are evocative of her sensibilities and her craftsmanship.

I was touched to learn that my own favourite sleeve cut, the raglan, was first designed by Aquascutum[1] for a Lord Raglan following his loss of his right arm. Although this felt a bit of a guilty pleasure – a titled military figure being served by an exclusive outfitter not being the most intersectional case study! – engaging with fashion also implies embracing the idiosyncracies of our personal tastes.

Even more important is the chapter devoted to disabled makers and designers. Like Earl Black, who dreams of colours at night and weaves those colours the next day at the Independence Association's Spindleworks in Maine. Annett-Hitchcock acknowledges that it is unknown how many disabled designers are working in fashion and hopes that this is the tip of the iceberg: either way, we need to improve both our understanding and the situation, the accessibility and inclusiveness of design education being another barrier. Again, this book contributes to both.

Taking our own meeting place of design and disability studies, Studio Ordinary, as an illustration, this book will inform our pragmatic, critical and speculative design practice: Andrew Cook designing inclusive lab coats the role of which is as much cultural – to assert one's place in the laboratory as a community – as it is practical; Katie Brown exploring nuance in hearing aid design with people who are deaf or hard of hearing – between the polarization of flesh-coloured plastic and diamond encrusting, by drawing on the materials of eyewear and the design philosophy of Naoto Fukasawa and Jasper Morrison.

And even when our work is not so obviously fashion-related, this historical analysis will still be a valuable resource across the time frames of past, present

---

[1] a moth-eaten Aquascutum raglan woollen coat that hangs in my shed has now doubled in significance and value to me. I will now not throw it away after all.

and near-future: Jessica Miller researching the erased histories of disabled designers who have too often been written out or re-cast as testers rather than creators – excluded not only in their lifetimes but from their own histories; Johanna Roehr and Fin Tams-Gray exploring alternative futures for augmented communication. Reflecting on Laurie Anderson's notion that technology is the campfire around which we tell our stories, then the stories we tell – the histories – affect the way we feed that fire and the way we shape the future of those technologies.

Graham Pullin
Studio Ordinary
Dundee, Scotland

About the Author

Kate Annett-Hitchcock, Ph.D., is a Professor at the Wilson College of Textiles, North Carolina State University, USA, where she teaches fashion design and development. Her research interests are user-focused fashion design and product development. She also has strong interests in fashion entrepreneurship and the history of all aspects of the industry. She is a proud graduate of three world-class institutions: The University of Manchester, Michigan State University and Virginia Tech. This is her first book.

Preface

I began my work with the intersection of fashion and disability during my first year of doctoral studies at Virginia Tech. My landlady was experiencing progressive post-polio syndrome, and continued to teach classes at the university as well as having her own practice as a potter. She hired me to make dresses for her based on a pattern from a dress she had bought in the UK. It got me thinking about how professional women with disabilities accessed work-appropriate clothing at an affordable price. I put aside my intended doctoral dissertation, which was something to do with the history of the textile economy, and turned my attention in a completely different direction.

After twenty years, I'm still astounded when people seem surprised to hear what I study, as if they hadn't thought about the fact that people with disabilities need to wear clothes. With training as an art historian, and a short stint in collections management and curatorial studies, I decided that it was time to take some of the legwork I had done in my dissertation and build on it to create a historical introduction to the topic. This soon turned into a research project with a vast array of fascinating stories, some of which are told here, and many of which have been put aside for future projects. After talking with curators and beginning the project just as the fashion industry is starting to reconcile with those it has "othered," it became evident that a history of fashion dealing exclusively with disability should become the focus of this work.

I feel that I have only started to scratch the surface of what is out there but I hope that what is laid out might be of interest and may help readers understand that self-expression and self-actualization through clothing and textiles are everyone's rights.

Acknowledgments

To my publisher Georgia Kennedy at Bloomsbury Visual Arts, a very heartfelt thanks for sticking with this project through Covid and other events over these three years, and for responding so quickly to my questions.

To my interviewees Anne Bissonnette, Sunae Park Evans, Lucy Jones, Grace Jun, Justin LeBlanc, and Alexandra Palmer, your words and insight were inspirational and your work is a critical part of this story.

To my colleagues at NC State: Cynthia Levine, Bertha Chang, and Greg Tourino of NC State Libraries; Meredith Jeffers of Wilson College of Textiles; Lu Liu and Christine Clocke of the College of Design; and Hector Jaimes, Professor of Spanish, you added some critical pieces of advice and practical help that enabled this book to come to fruition.

To the multiple curatorial and museum staff in North America whose collections and organizations were instrumental in turning up evidence for this project, thank you: Vlada Blinova, University of Alberta; Adrienne Saint-Pierre, The Barnum Museum; Michelle McVicker and Emma McClendon, The Museum at FIT; Nicola Woods, Royal Ontario Museum; Katherine Ott, National Museum of American History; Marci Morimoto, The Metropolitan Museum of Art; Jennifer Byram, Choctaw Nation; Tracey Panek, Levi Strauss & Co.; Karen Morse, University of Rhode Island; Edith Serkownek, Sara Hume, and Cara Gilgenbach, Kent State University; and Gayle Strege, The Ohio State University.

To the folks in the UK who gave me important information and in some cases hosted me in exploring their collections: Clara Morgan, Sheffield Museums Trust; Miles Lambert, Platt Hall; Anthea Godfrey, Embroiders' Guild, UK; Will Phillips, Bucks County Museum; Claire Allen-Johnstone and Susan North, Victoria and Albert Museum; Louise Price, George Marshall Medical

Museum; Rebecca Ellison, Claydon House; John Peel, Manchester Art Gallery; Rada Vlatkovic, Wellcome Collection; and Georgina Ripley, National Museums Scotland.

To librarians and archivists on both sides of the Atlantic who have been so generous with their time, expertise and hospitality: Brooke Guthrie of Duke University's David M. Rubenstein Rare Book & Manuscript Library; Tim Knebel of Sheffield City Archives; Mike Shadix of Roosevelt Warm Springs; and Paul Friedman, The New York Public Library.

To all who generously helped with access to images: Billy Price of Billy Footwear; Emma Rutherford of Philip Mould & Company; Glenda S. Barahona of NYU Medical Archives and Special Collections; Earl Black and Brian Braley of Spindleworks of Independence Association; Dee Cankaya of Lock & Co.; Cindy Mackey of Harvard University's Peabody Museum of Archaeology and Ethnology; and Stephanie Lake.

Finally, there are many additional people who have impacted this work in so many ways, some over many years, generously giving their expertise and knowledge when I besieged them with questions: Mark D. Hutter; Linda Baumgarten; Nicole Belolan; Ladies of the Junior League of Charlotte, NC; Sandra Hutton; Denise Green; Suzanne Boudjada; Joseph McBrinn; Kate Strasdin; Jean Druesedow; Eleri Lynn Ritchie; Nathan Arndt; D.A. Saguto; Lesley Edwards; Natalie Wright; Graham Pullin; Debbie Myers; Ellen Braaten; Doris Kincade, Julia Beamish, and Paige Moore. You are all part of this work and what is yet to come.

Funding for research travel for this book was provided by The Pasold Research Fund; The Colleen Callahan Professional Development Award, Costume Society of America Southeastern Region; and The Ellen Rohde Leadership Initiative Professional Development Grant, NC State University.

Abbreviations

ADA	Americans with Disabilities Act
ADL	Activities of Daily Living
CDC	Centers for Disease Control and Prevention
ICF	International Classification of Functioning, Disability and Health
WHO	World Health Organization
UNCRPD	United Nations Convention on the Rights of Persons with Disabilities
USDA	United States Department of Agriculture

Glossary

All definitions from Merriam-Webster online dictionary, except for *
which are author-generated and ** where otherwise referenced in
Glossary Notes.

Fashion-Related Terms

Bicorne a hat with a brim turned up on two sides and worn either front to back or sideways

Gros-point embroidery made with large stitches each of which crosses two vertical and
two horizontal threads [of the base fabric]

Petit-point a short stitch slanting upwards to the right that is used in embroidery to form
even lines of solid background (also known as tent stitch)

Corset a close-fitting boned supporting undergarment that is often hooked and laced and
that extends from above or beneath the bust or from the waist to below the hips

Cotton calico plain weave mid-weight cotton fabric originally imported from India

Doffing to remove (an article of clothing) from the body

Donning to put on (an article of clothing)

*****Fashion industry** the entire supply chain bringing fashion articles to the consumer,
encompassing designing, production and processing of fiber, fabric, clothing, and
distribution through wholesale and retail outlets, plus branding and marketing activities

*****Patternmaking** the art and science of creating a two-dimensional simulation of part of
an item of clothing, which can then be cut from material and fitted to a three-
dimensional object, such as the human body

Seamstress a woman whose occupation is sewing (a male of the same occupation is
referred to as a seamster, but tailor is more commonly used)

****Stays** earlier term for corset made very rigid with iron or whalebone. Made like a bodice
laced up back with scoop neckline in front, higher in back, with shoulder straps set
wide in front[1]

Tailor a person whose occupation is making or altering garments (such as suits, jackets,
and dresses) typically to fit a particular person

*****Western/industrialized fashion** the Eurocentric approach to fashion, which according to
fashion historians began in fourteenth-century royal circles. This format gained
traction during the colonial era and expanded during the nineteenth century; this is
the modern industrial fashion complex we currently experience

Other Terms

References for each provided separately.

Activities of daily living: a term used to collectively describe fundamental skills required to independently care for oneself, such as mobility, bathing, and eating. These are often used to measure aspects of disability and rehabilitation.[2]

Cooperative extension: an arm of the USDA formally established by the Smith Lever Act of 1914 to provide agricultural education to farmers in the US, generate research and share information[3]

Land-grant universities: American institutions of higher education established as a result of the Morrill Act in 1862. Each US state at that time received land and funding so that agriculture and engineering could be taught to meet the need of the nation's rapidly increasing industries and population.[4] Land-grant universities served as the site of cooperative extension activities (see above)

Rehabilitation: a process whereby an individual participates in improving or regaining an aspect of quality of life that has been lost or diminished in some way through congenital defect, injury, illness, or disease, whether permanent or temporary. Contemporary rehabilitation practice involves a rehabilitation team including occupational therapists, rehabilitation nurses, physical therapists, and counseling psychologists working together to ensure reintegration of the individual into desired social and cultural circles and to improve quality of life.[5]

Universal design: the design of products and environments to be usable by all people, to the greatest extent possible, without the need for adaptation or specialized design.[6]

Glossary Notes

1   Calasibetta, C. M. & Tortora, P. (2003), *The Fairchild Dictionary of Fashion*, 3rd edition, New York, NY: Fairchild Publications, Inc.

2   Katz S. (1983), "Assessing self-maintenance: activities of daily living, mobility, and instrumental activities of daily living", *Journal of the American Geriatric Society*, 31 (12): 721–7.

3   USDA National Institute of Food and Agriculture (2022), *Cooperative Extension History*. Available online: https://www.nifa.usda.gov/about-nifa/how-we-work/extension/cooperative-extension-history (accessed December 29, 2022).

4   Brittanica.com (2022), *Land-grant universities*. Available online: https://www.britannica.com/topic/land-grant-university (accessed December 29, 2022).

5   Kottke, F. J. (1982), "Philosophic considerations of quality of life for the disabled", *Archives of Physicians Medical Rehabilitation*, 63 (2): 60–2.

6   North Carolina State University College of Design (2022). *Center for Universal Design.* Available online: https://design.ncsu.edu/research/center-for-universal-design/ (accessed December 26, 2022).

1

Establishing Significance

Introduction

This chapter serves as an introduction to the book and its structure. It also outlines the approach taken—the construction of a disability fashion history that can set the context for developments that are taking place in the contemporary fashion industry. This history, which is presented in a traditional chronological format, highlights developments that have silently coexisted alongside mainstream Western/industrialized fashion, and culminates in an examination of the contemporary rise in fashion inclusivity on a global scale. The chapter explains what is included and what is left out, together with rationales for both. An overview of the medical and social models of disability is provided for contextual understanding, and the vocabulary of both disability and fashion are discussed and framed. The chapter outlines some of the disciplines that were utilized in the research process for the book and gives a glimpse of some of the main characters and innovators who have contributed to the historical narrative.

1.1 Purpose of the Book: It's a Fashion Story!

This book was conceived and written to address aspects of the shifting patterns in the global fashion industry's awareness of the civil rights of disabled consumers—specifically, the right to participate in the world of fashion as creators, consumers and activists. As a professional participant in the contemporary academic fashion ecosystem and a trained fashion historian, I—a non-disabled white British academic based in the United States—felt that the time was right for a high-level historical observation and analysis of the intersection of fashion and disability from a variety of perspectives. Above all, I felt this needed to be set within a historical context, to help bring current developments into perspective and open dialogue for awareness and understanding.

While the mainstream fashion industry has been a relative latecomer to the table when it comes to including the disabled consumer in product and distribution activities, academic interest in "clothing for the disabled" has existed for several decades as a research topic in home economics, fashion design and rehabilitation-related disciplines, with an ebb and flow that is partially linked to government funding priorities. In recent years, however, interest has accelerated and resulted in an increased number of research articles in a wide variety of academic journals. In a study on the frequency of papers published on this topic since 1990, Esmail et al. (2020) found that 50 percent of studies have been conducted since 2009, with 30 percent of these studies occurring in fashion and apparel-related literature (as compared to rehabilitation literature, medical literature and other non-fashion fields).[1] However, the availability and access to fashion products at the consumer/retail level has experienced slower growth than the academic research interest and output. Only since around 2010 have practical solutions and strategies for inclusivity begun to take root in the global mass-market fashion industry, precipitated by public awareness, advances in design and production technologies, marketing, and distribution strategies that help us think beyond the possible into the realms of the probable.

This book is structured to begin setting the stage for readers who seek a broad historical background within which to contextualize these developments. The world of mass fashion as the industry we know today has existed for approximately 180 years, but peoples' need to be fashionable is a much older form of self-expression and fulfills a sense of belonging to social and cultural structures. As Susan Kaiser states: "The process of fashioning bodies is more than just a white, Western, Heterosexual, bourgeois female consumer affair. Indeed, fashion highlights the multiple intersections and entanglements among gender, race, ethnicity, national identity, social class, sexuality, and other facts of our identities." (Kaiser 2012: 4).[2] The history of the fashioning of our bodies has been very well-documented and studied, but only for the "white,

Figure 1.1 *Model, athlete and double amputee Aimee Mullins. Aimee Mullins walks the runway during the Alexander McQueen Ready to Wear Spring/Summer 1999 fashion show as part of London Fashion Week on September 27, 1998 in London, United Kingdom. Photo by Victor VIRGILE/Gamma-Rapho via Getty Images*

Western" consumer described by Kaiser. As this book will demonstrate, disabled consumers have always existed, no matter the cultural/historical setting, and the desire of all people to fashion their appearance as a form of self-expression deserves to be acknowledged and understood.

In Western and/or industrialized societies, one can argue that access to fashion has always been exclusionary; limited to the wealthy and entitled as a way of setting themselves apart from less fortunate fellow citizens. However, despite the gradual democratization of fashion throughout the twentieth century, when the effects of the Industrial Revolution and capitalism allowed access to desirable products at more affordable price points, enabling many more consumers to live a fashionable lifestyle, little progress has been made to be inclusive of marginalized groups who have been left outside the gates of the fashionable world. Even in the 1950s and 1960s, when the first attempts were made to bring the work of established fashion designers together under one label (Helen Cookman's Functional Fashions), the impact on the global fashion industry remained minimal until the early twenty-first century.[3] An example of work done under the Functional Fashions label can be seen in Figs 1.2 a and b.

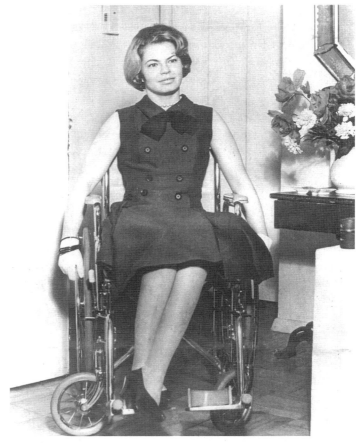

Figures 1.2 a and b *(Continued).*

Figures 1.2 a and b *A dress "Approved for design by the Clothing Research and Development Foundation (Functional Fashions label) by Shannon Rodgers for Jerry Silverman" (c. 1965), shown on both a seated model and a standing model. The garment is a sleeveless, dark-colored, double-breasted front shift-style dress with a bow at the front neck. The seated model is shown in front of some flowers, while the standing model is shown in front of a bookcase. Photo Credit: Marian Stephenson, (Photos from Helen Cookman, Exec. Director of C.R.D.F., 48 e. 66 St, NYC 21)*

Throughout history, the job of providing fashionable and accessible clothing has been left largely to creative individuals, independent designers and enterprising companies working outside the mainstream to address individual consumer needs. The common thread has typically been proximity to or personal experience with disability, a significant factor that affects almost every development examined in this book. I write in part to highlight their efforts and to explore recent progress in inclusion of disabled consumers in the global fashion conversation through inclusivity strategies.

The book touches on another issue confronting fashion—whether the act of being fashionable throughout history has actively contributed to the act of being disabled. The research shows that the two worlds have experienced some complex relationships over the years through specific items of clothing. The corset, as an example, has existed as a means of re-shaping the human body to a predetermined fashionable silhouette over centuries, but it has also done duty as an orthopedic device, dating back to an initial development by a French surgeon in the sixteenth century. The irony here, of course, is that while this garment shaped the "deformed" body into a "straight" posture because of intervention by a concerned male medical professional, it was at the same time being used to fashionably "deform" the natural shape of the body (men, women and children) into something very artificial with potential health consequences. Historical texts from the seventeenth century onwards show the duality of correction and disguise being the primary goals behind invention and production of devices marketed towards people with a "deformity," thus culturally adapting a body to conform to norms of beauty and fashion at any given period.

The book will show how, in the latter part of the twentieth century, fashion started to move from hiding disability to revealing it, due in part to the civil rights and independence movements, together with government legislation and subsequent changes in public policy. An example of this can be found in recent developments in prosthetics. This topic has been well documented and discussed elsewhere, so it will not be a focus of this book, but suffice to say that these originally purely functional products, painted in the nineteenth century to resemble the replaced body part as closely as possible, have today been elevated to the forefront of aesthetic expression and technological progress. Prosthetic designers and manufacturers create products that are worn visibly and proudly. In many ways, disability is responsible for birthing fashion items out of the prosthetic and assistive technology realm to become status symbols.[4] Because of this aspect of the relationship between fashion and disability, I hope to present a case for how fashion can be an effective advocate in presenting and promoting cultural change towards inclusivity and acceptance of all bodies, no matter their appearance, size, shape or ability.

Fashion is a human phenomenon; the desire of human beings to self-fashion impacts lives through cultural acceptance and self-expression. However, the historical navigation of fashion and disability conducted for this book shows that the language used for exploring both topics presents challenges and at times throughout history has been offensive. For this book, fashion is defined as products worn on the body through which human beings non-verbally communicate a defined cultural aesthetic. The terms "Clothing," "Apparel," "Garments," "Attire," "Garb," "Raiment," among others, have all been used interchangeably for such products in historical studies.[5] A similar challenge presented itself in defining disability, the various models of which will be explored later in this chapter. Terminology surrounding disability, even today, is continually developing. I have selected the term "disabled" to describe consumers, users of products, designers and the myriad of individuals who have been marginalized by fashion throughout history. With respect to other terms that are currently in use, such as "people with disabilities," the decision was made to use the word "disabled" as a descriptor to emphasize the environmental aspect of disability. In other words, to show that a person is as disabled as their environment allows. In addition, following the practice of engaging advisors from the community, the term "disabled" was verified as being appropriate for use in this book.

Beginning the journey of historical research necessitated the formation of a list of search terms and keywords. In doing so, I quickly discovered that in order to carry out a full search of primary resources, terminology such as "Cripple," "Handicap," "Defective," "Deformity," "Monster," and other items, needed to be included.[6] In addition, the search was constrained to include only physical disability, meaning that there was no exploration of the relationship between fashion and cognitive or learning disabilities. Obesity and aging were also excluded from this work (even though some US states consider obesity to be a disability and the condition therefore falls under the Americans with Disability Act for purposes of anti-discrimination lawsuits). Both these topics demand attention but involve more space, time and interdisciplinary research than is possible in this book.

Another important item that will facilitate author/reader transparency is the choice to limit the scope of the book to Western/industrialized fashion and Western/industrialized models of disability. Currently 40 percent of the academic and popular literature about the intersection of fashion and disability emanates from the United States; therefore, there is geographical bias for a significant portion of the twentieth century and contemporary discussions. The earlier historical research, although broadened to reflect traditional models of Western fashion history, is still confined to a Eurocentric and American perspective due to time and financial constraints. The historical journey begins in the Northern European Renaissance period, with the caveat there is a wealth of untapped information to be explored in non-Western fashion and disability paradigms. For example, of great interest for future research but out of the scope of this book is what can be learned from the attitude towards pre-contact people in the Americas and how they facilitated clothing and self-expression. Kim Nielsen, in her excellent book about the history of disability in the United States, explains how indigenous peoples believed that "every person and thing has a gift (a skill, ability, purpose). When individuals, communities, and the world are in harmony, individuals, often with the help of others, find and embrace their gifts and put them into practice." (Nielsen 2013: 5)[7]

The research for this book has spanned many disciplines in addition to Fashion History, including: rehabilitation; engineering; medicine; economics; and politics, to name a few. Those who are familiar with the diversity of fashion studies understand the complex nature of documenting fashion when it intersects with other disciplines. The diversity of primary and secondary resources needed to gain a fuller picture of the topic is vast and this book has only scratched the surface of the possibilities that are apparent with a multidisciplinary approach.

Finally, the primary goal of this book from its initial conception has always been to document the history of the intersection of fashion and disability in order to set current developments in context. It is important to acknowledge the history of products and people whose lives have impacted the field and have contributed to its development. To ignore this would be disingenuous to the innovative and creative advances that have been made throughout history and would exclude context towards inclusivity in contemporary fashion.

Ignoring this history would have meant losing a wealth of important information. Too often, contemporary society believes that, due to advances in technology, contemporary practice contains all the answers. I argue through historical primary and secondary research that this is not always the case. Historical detective work repeatedly elicited examples about ingenious adaptations made to fashionable garments by unidentified tailors and seamstresses so that human bodies could be accommodated into the world of fashion. It was also important to include stories of disabled makers, adding an element to the discourse that was as impactful as it was unexpected. The entrepreneurial spirit of independent designers and small businesses who pioneered techniques and independent living will shine through as the foundations of today's success stories. I hope that all these stories combined with new perspectives on how fashion has interacted with disability will bring new knowledge and meaning to readers and open up pathways of thinking and working to move this topic forward.

1.2 Medical and Social Models of Disability

At this point, some definition regarding the model of disability that guides this book is necessary for context. There are many ways of looking at how both disability and fashion can be defined, so this approach can co-exist alongside many others and can be thought about, discussed and debated in light of the facts. At the time of writing, 26 percent of Americans (CDC 2020) and about 15 percent of the global population (Worldbank.org 2021) live with some kind of disability, equating to one out of every four people in the US and over one billion people worldwide.[8] [9] Physical disability is just one aspect of the overall disability conversation, and its relationship to fashion is the focus of this book. Physical disability, comprising just one segment of all disabilities, affects millions of people on a global level and ranges in severity from minor problems with occasional pain to incapacitation involving the loss or loss of use of one or more limbs.

The concept of disability has been identified, defined and measured in many ways, due to the diverse nature of its various internal and external manifestations within the human body. Conceptual clarity has been fundamental to the development of a working theoretical base for clothing research. There has been no shortage of guidance from the public healthcare field for those looking for definitions. The US Centers for Disease Control and Prevention (CDC 2020) define disability as follows: "A disability is any condition of the body or mind (impairment) that makes it more difficult for the person with the condition to do certain activities (activity limitation) and interact with the world around them (participation restrictions)."[10] The CDC definition thus focuses on a specific condition and its impact on the individual within society.

The Americans with Disabilities Act (ADA), which remains the most recent piece of significant US legislation aimed at improving the quality of life for Americans who are disabled, defines disability as "(1) a physical or mental impairment that substantially limits one or more major life activities, (2) a record of having such an impairment, or (3) being regarded as having such an impairment."[11] The language of the ADA demonstrates the degree of openness for variance in interpretation, but also focuses on the impairment or condition, and how that restricts or limits activity.

The World Health Organization's (WHO) International Classification of Functioning, Disability and Health (ICF), is more fluid and contextual, acknowledging the part that environment plays in a disabling condition. The ICF refrains from formally defining disability but provides a classification system, noting on its homepage: "As the functioning and disability of an individual occurs in a context, ICF also includes a list of environmental factors. ICF is the WHO framework for measuring health and disability at both individual and population levels. ICF was officially endorsed by all 191 WHO Member States in the Fifty-fourth World Health Assembly on 22 May 2001 (resolution WHA 54.21) as the international standard to describe and measure health and disability."[12] The ICF checklist, a form that can be downloaded from the website and is intended for "use by a clinician, health or social care professional," is designed to "elicit and record information on the functioning and disability of an individual." Part two of the checklist, which gathers information about activity and participation in "life situations," lists "Dressing" under "Self-care" (code d540) and "Shopping" under "Domestic Life" (code d620). Other categories exist where the implicit questioning could certainly relate to self-fashioning activities. By introducing environmental factors, the ICF definition implies that although disability might manifest at the individual's physical level, it then expands to affect broader aspects of human performance, impacting an individual's interaction with society and the environment (WHO 2021).

These different ways of thinking about disability are typically categorized as the *medical* and *social* models. The medical model of disability tends to focus on the individual person and their clinical diagnosis, whereas the social model focuses on an individual's environment and their ability to function within those environmental constraints. Both models of disability can guide us towards a deeper understanding about how people with disabilities might or might not be able to connect with designed products and services in the multiple environments within which they negotiate daily life. But additionally, the social model conveys the idea that disability can be perceived as a continuum where there are context-specific, not absolute, levels of abilities for an individual. Rosemarie Garland-Thomson (1997), discussing the Western/industrialized perspective that disability is the opposite of able-bodiedness, suggests that: "Disability cancels out other qualities, reducing the complex person to a single attribute." (Garland-Thomson 1997: 4)[13] It is my goal in this book to demonstrate how fashion embraces and enhances the whole person through its own unique complexities, which are also context-specific.

The ICF definition integrates both the medical and social approaches because it represents "a coherent view of different perspectives of health: biological, individual and social." (ICF 2002: 9).[14] Social limitations (such as an inability to access retail stores and purchase fashion products) incorporate restrictions created by society. Barriers which restrict achievement of self-actualization (such as inadequate or inaccessible clothing for the workplace) can also be thought of in this way. Once an individual interacts with, and becomes limited by, their ability to function in society, the disability (both problem and solution) moves from the person to the environment. Clothing and fashion can be seen as a part of the environment—the environment that most closely surrounds an individual—and therefore operate as a facilitator of social functioning and currency within the greater environment. Bubolz, Eicher and Sontag (1979) referred to this as the Human Constructed Environment (HCE) in their groundbreaking work on the human ecosystem. They state: "Clothing illustrates the interrelationship of the HCE's three components [socio-physical, socio-biological, socio-cultural]. The domesticated animal or cultivated plant is converted by tool-using humans into fabrics for garments whose use is governed by social norms and customs as well as by the natural condition of climate and geography."[15] (Bubolz, Eicher and Sontag 1979: 30). To return to ICF language: "Environmental factors make up the physical, social and attitudinal environment in which people live and conduct their lives." (ICF 2002: 10)[16]

These and other similar perspectives have led me to the awareness that disability as a construct is a result of exclusionary policies and lack of discourse, rather than an objective physical state. Both these problems, while embedded within Western/industrialized society, are not insurmountable and it is my argument that fashion actually provides a bridge that can be used for discourse between Western/industrialized society and those who it has "othered," through a shared interest in self-expression. As Julia Twigg states: "There is a long history according to which subordinated groups—women, black people—are represented in terms of their bodies, effectively reducing them to their bodies." (Twigg 2013: 41).[17] Fashion provides the means by which bodies can be represented and brought to the same cultural playing field.

1.3 Framing of Disability Fashion History

As previously mentioned, the history of Western/industrialized fashion is well documented and disseminated in academic and public arenas. Museums across the world count fashion exhibits among their biggest crowd pullers. Period dramas on television and in the movie industry are often referred to as costume dramas. Western/industrialized fashion history sells in many areas. However, venturing outside of this traditional perspective of fashion history, there is a serious lack of coverage regarding bodies of fashion that are differently shaped or abled. This problem prompted the decision to devote a large portion of this book to historical research and perhaps even begin to build a Disability Fashion History so that the historical deficit can be addressed. As Liz Linthicum states: "Logic suggests that there has always been a history of clothing that has evolved around people who have been determined as 'disabled.'" (Linthicum 2006: 309).[18]

The exact nature of how this research was planned and how parts of the story were discovered and pieced together is detailed at the beginning of ch. 2. It is exciting to be able to begin building a new perspective and I am hopeful that a new line of analysis will open up within the traditional fashion history, which for so long has been a story of abled entitled people. Even though a formal disability fashion history has yet to be written, it is important to note that disabled people have often been historical fashion icons, whether or not their disability was concealed or revealed. In order to tell a few of these stories, a portion of the book is devoted to presenting profiles of some of these figures, such as Lavinia Warren (Fig. 1.3), wife of General Tom Thumb, who was part of P.T. Barnum's Circus in the nineteenth century, and a client of both Charles Frederick Worth, the renowned French couturier and Madame Demorest, the famous New York City designer and dressmaker.

Figure 1.3 *Lavinia Warren Stratton wearing checked dress, holding fan, c.1870–76. Lavinia is shown holding a fan and posed sideways to show off her fashionable early bustle and train. Photographed by Vandyke and Brown, Liverpool, England. Photo Credit: Barnum Museum, Bridgeport, Connecticut*

The scant attention paid to disabled bodies in fashion history is not unusual considering how little historical research in general has interacted with disability. Museums have grappled with how to represent the disenfranchised whose stories have mostly been written and told by others. Annie Delin (2002) writes:

> Within museums, disabled people might not find a single image of a person like themselves—no affirmation that in the past people like themselves lived, worked, created great art, wore clothes, were loved or esteemed. If they do see an image of someone exactly like themselves and seek to know more about them, there is a chance that their name is missing from the catalogue or label—that they are known as "the dwarf", "the giant", "a marvel of nature". Similarly, works of art *by* disabled people are characterised by absence of information which would allow onlookers to learn that the work was created by a disabled person ... Disabled history can in this sense be regarded as part of a phenomenon known as "hidden history".
>
> DELIN, 2002: 84[19]

This book, as the first attempt at a disability fashion history, should be seen somewhat as a practice dive, meant to be built on, and offered up for discussion, debate and hopefully much more investigation. Finding primary and secondary resources, as described in ch. 2, is challenging, and the process is certainly not linear. The information gathered was obtained slowly and with the incredible help of many curators and scholars, especially for the early historical data retrieval prior to 1900. Documentation of initiatives and programs in the post-First World War era, such as the use of clothing in the 1920s by professionals as a self-help or rehabilitation tool, was more accessible. The search became even easier for material from the post-Second World War era, due in part to recognition of the need for fashion to be made available to disabled consumers, which created a greater amount of initiatives and public recognition. These included formalized research programs, service organizations, academic publications, organizations and entrepreneurial small businesses.

The book includes profiles of fashion icons such as Lavinia Warren and Frida Kahlo, and descriptions of the pioneering work of disabled creators such as Annie Carter, who founded Painted Fabrics, Inc., (Fig. 1.4) and Ernest

Figure 1.4 *Painted Fabrics' brochure cover for a sale. Painted Fabrics is written in an ornamental style above an illustration of a woman in a purple and blue dress. Information about sales in London, Harrogate and Sheffield at the lower part of the brochure cover. Photo Credit: Sheffield Libraries and Archives: PF/1/2*

Thesiger, founder of the Disabled Soldiers Embroidery Industry, both established in Great Britain and emerging from craft therapy programs set up during the First World War. But there are stories that this book does not have the scope to tell, such as contemporary movements which are fashion-related (for example, the Queercrip movement exemplified by Sky Cubacub's Rebirth company). These important movements are impacting cultural change on a meta level in addition to their part in the global fashion industry. There are also many topics that will not be discussed as they have been well-researched in fields beyond fashion, such as practices which have only served to disable people's bodies (foot binding, scarification, and tight corseting, to name a few). Instead the focus is on the people who have simply wanted to live with fashion while also being disabled. The book will attempt to tell the story of their contribution to today's fashion accessibility narrative.

The book will approach the historical intersectionality of disability and fashion in the traditional chronological method adopted by mainstream surveys of Western fashion history. In the final chapter, a Disability Fashion History timeline will be presented to show the significant events that are discussed throughout the book. The text will shed light on the achievements made to assist all bodies in a fashionable way of life. At times the chapters will contain overlap with medical literature and technological developments, but it is my view that the act of fashioning our bodies for self and/or social expression involves many processes and approaches.

The book will also look at contemporary design and possible future pathways. Recent years have witnessed major changes in the intersection of fashion and disability. It is important to take a brief look at these changes and how they have impacted this intersection. Developments in design, technology, social media marketing, and distribution over the past decade have precipitated accessibility in many areas, not just disability. There is a generational awareness and push to include all bodies in the room and at the table, in a concerted effort to make the fashion world less exclusionary.

Summary

The disabled community have had decisions made on their behalf for a very long time—by medical practitioners, school systems, government, and the environments in which they live. The freedom that fashion allows individuals to express themselves in diverse ways gives agency over the body and how we present it to the world. Fashion gives confidence—not just for who we are but who we might want to be. Fashion is an outward manifestation of personal expression within the context of cultural and social milieus, and above all, fashion is fun!

This disabled fashion history tells the story of the tension between the conceal and reveal intentionality apparent in fashion. Western society has not always been kind to the visibly disabled person (Garland-Thomson's *opposite of abled* comes to mind from earlier in this chapter) and there have even been instances in the United States where laws were passed targeting and discriminating against the disabled in public spaces.[20] Designers and wearers still negotiate whether "adapted" clothing should visually embrace or hide disability. In the accessories and assistive devices arena, there have been efforts made to lead the way in standing out, such as brightly colored canes, "glammed out" wheelchairs, and beautifully decorated prosthetics. Even assistive devices that are very much a part of the lexicon of mainstream life, such as eyeglasses, represent individuality with their variety and a way of transforming and creating the fashionable self. Luxury-oriented companies such as FFORA, which is making wheelchair accessories fashionable, desirable, and accessible, are helping cross boundaries and promoting inclusivity for multiple consumers.

Fashion retailers are labeling their products with the term "adaptive," and in this book, that will be the language used to describe contemporary fashion. In terms of product mix, "adaptive" fashion startups are rapidly evolving new and innovative ideas, much in the tradition of the small family businesses of the 1960s and 1970s, except in this case, accompanied by the polished marketing, creative websites and powerful social media campaigns to push their products out to the people who really need them. One example of this would be Slick Chicks, which specializes in underwear for women who have trouble navigating traditional undergarments. Established brands like Tommy Hilfiger and Zappos count the adaptive market as part of their product and marketing mix, and pioneers such as Izzy Camelleri, who pivoted her existing business model to focus on the needs of people with disabilities with the legendary IzzyAdaptive brand, is now considered an important part of the adaptive fashion story.

Fashion stylists and advocates are empowering people with disabilities to take the fashioning of their bodies into their own hands with the least amount of inconvenience through YouTube videos and social media, using brands available in the mainstream marketplace. In the front and center world of fashion modeling, models such as Madeline Stuart and Aaron Rose Philip are breaking the mold in terms of expectations for fashion model inclusion, not only with their disability but also the breaking down of gender barriers.

Finally, at the time of writing, social media is driving change. Much of the social activism that has taken place over the last few years is instigated by people on the street communicating on a few online platforms, not by big companies pushing products through traditional marketing methods. Activism around fashion inclusion has increased to the point that the big brands are scrambling to be included. Accessible fashion, climate change activism, #BlackLivesMatter, #MeToo, and the tools in current use, such as TikTok, have all become agents of necessary discord that is needed to bring about self-examination in the fashion industry. Content creators are driving people to unashamedly claim their place at the fashion table. When the good for the minority becomes indispensable for the majority, then real change starts to occur. And as always, it's a fashion story first.

Notes

1   Esmail, A., Poncet, F., Auger, C., Rochette, A., Dahan-Oliel, N., Labbé, D., Kehayia, E., Billebaud, C., de Guise, E., Lessard, I., Ducharme, I., Vermeersch, O. and Swaine, B. (2020), "The role of clothing on participation of persons with a physical disability: A scoping review", *Applied Ergonomics*, 85: 1–15.

2   Kaiser, S. (2012), *Fashion & Cultural Studies*, London: Berg, reprinted by Bloomsbury 2013.

3   The "Functional Fashions" label, started by Helen Cookman and Muriel Zimmerman in the late 1950s in New York City will be discussed in more detail in ch. 4. Functional Fashions has also been studied in depth by Natalie Wright, see Wright, N.E. (2022), "Functional Fashions for the Physically Handicapped": Disability and Dress in Postwar America, *Dress*, 48 (2). (10.1080/03612112.2022.2090724).

4   See the discussion about luxury brand eyeglasses in Graham Pullin's book *Design meets disability*, as a good example of this argument. Pullin, G. (2009), *Design meets disability*, Cambridge MA: The MIT Press.

5   For a full discussion of terminology used in global fashion history studies, see "Chapter Two—The Lexicon of Fashion", in Welters, L. and Lillethun, A. (2018), *Fashion History: A Global View*, 13–29, London: Bloomsbury.

6   Subject headings used in the dictionary catalogs of the Library of Congress. Washington, DC: Govt. printing office, Library branch, 1st Edn, Library of Congress, Catalog Division.

7   Nielsen, K. (2013), *A Disability History of the United States*, Boston: Beacon Press.

8   Centers for Disease Control and Prevention (CDC) (2020), "Disability Impacts All of Us". Available online: https://www.cdc.gov/ncbddd/disabilityandhealth/documents/ disabilities_impacts_all_of_us.pdf (accessed December 21, 2022).

9   Worldbank.org (2022), "Disability Inclusion". Available online: https://www.worldbank. org/en/topic/disability#1 (accessed December 21, 2022).

10 Centers for Disease Control and Prevention (CDC), (2020), "Disability and Health Overview". Available online: https://www.cdc.gov/ncbddd/disabilityandhealth/ disability.html#:~:text=A%20disability%20is%20any%20condition,around%20 them%20(participation%20restrictions (accessed November 1, 2022).

11 ADA.gov (n.d.), Introduction to the Americans with Disabilities Act. Available online: https://www.ada.gov/ada_intro.htm (accessed November 1, 2022).

12 World Health Organization (2021), "International Classification of Functioning, Disability and Health (ICF)". Available online: https://www.who.int/standards/classifications/international-classification-of-functioning-disability-and-health (accessed November 1, 2022).

13 Garland-Thomson, R. (1997), *Extraordinary Bodies: Figuring Physical Disability in American Culture and Literature*, New York: Columbia University Press.

14 ICF (2002), "Towards a Common Language for Functioning, Disability and Health, Geneva: World Health Organization". Available online: https://cdn.who.int/media/docs/default-source/classification/icf/icfbeginnersguide.pdf?sfvrsn=eead63d3_4&download=true (accessed November 1, 2022).

15 Bubolz, M., Eicher, J. and Sontag, M.S. (1979), "The human ecosystem: a model", *Journal of Home Economics*, 71 (1): 28–31.

16 ICF (2002), "Towards a Common Language for Functioning, Disability and Health, Geneva: World Health Organization". Available online: https://cdn.who.int/media/docs/default-source/classification/icf/icfbeginnersguide.pdf?sfvrsn=eead63d3_4&download=true (accessed November 1, 2022).

17 Twigg, J. (2013), *Fashion and Age: Dress, the Body and Later Life*, London: Bloomsbury Academic.

18 Linthicum, L. (2006), "Integrative Practice: Oral History, Dress and Disability Studies", *Journal of Design History*, 19 (4): 309–18.

19 Delin, A. (2002), "Buried in the Footnotes: The Absence of Disabled People in the Collective Imagery of our Past", in R. Sandell (ed), *Museums, Society, Inequality*, 84–97, London: Routledge.

20 See Susan M. Schweik's *The Ugly Laws: Disability in Public*, (2009), part of the History of Disability series edited by Paul K. Longmore and Lauri Umansky, published by New York University Press.

2

Underpinnings: Events Prior to 1800

Introduction

This chapter provides the first segment of historical context for the discourse between disability and fashion. Beginning with the Renaissance and ending at the end of the eighteenth century, evidence has been selected to show how fashionable clothing was adapted and altered to conceal and sometimes "cure" disability, built on the premise of the medical model referred to in ch. 1, that disabled people were to be "cured" of their "disease." Primary and secondary sources for this research came mostly from the US and from Western Europe— unfortunately it is outside the scope of this book to move beyond the Western/ industrialized fashion paradigm. Included are fashion items that have been adapted to fit disabled bodies; inventions designed to "correct" the fashionable body, and stories of some fashionable people whose disabilities elicited some creative design responses. Also included is some perspective from museum professionals discussing the challenges of mounting historic exhibits focusing on fashion and disability.

2.1 Setting the Stage for the Historical Discussion

It is my belief that current discourse on any topic must acknowledge and build on historic precedent in order to fully understand its contemporary context.

The history of Western/industrialized fashion has been well researched and formally documented by academics, designers, independent scholars and museum professionals, as well as informally by many others, such as commentators, bloggers, etc. Outcomes of this body of work range from general surveys of fashion to monographs on a focused topic or specific designer, as well as hands-on practical information, such as guidelines for re-enactment costumes and technical directives for the performing arts. Museums around the world count exhibits which focus on fashion and adornment among their biggest "blockbusters," including the Metropolitan Museum in New York City, whose 2011 show, "Alexander McQueen: Savage Beauty," drew 661,509 visitors (MetMuseum.org 2011).[1] This made it one of the most visited shows in the museum's history, with people standing in line for nearly four hours to see it on the closing day (Hollander 2011).[2] The history of the intersection of fashion and disability has been less rigorously explored, documented and showcased. Like many aspects of disability, the way that disabled people have fashioned their world has been largely ignored as an area of study and documentation. Anne Bissonnette, Associate Professor and Curator of the Clothing and Textiles Collection at the University of Alberta, explains that: "Most of what has been collected is 'the ideal.'"[3] This chapter seeks to fill in some of the gaps and explore reasons for this omission by the history books. I hope to show how the history of "disabled" fashion has existed alongside abled and Western/industrialized society, but in a concealed, disguised and in some cases, misinterpreted way.

Historical texts, in telling the stories of human societies and their created cultures, have tended to omit disability issues because they have not sat comfortably within the traditional storytelling of some nations. Kim Nielsen (2013) explains the situation as follows within the context of U.S. history:

> Throughout U.S. history, disability has been used symbolically and metaphorically in venues as diverse as popular culture (19th century freak shows) and language ("That's so lame"; "What a retard"; "special"). When "disability" is considered to be synonymous with "deficiency" and "dependency", it contrasts sharply with American ideals of independence and autonomy.
>
> NIELSEN 2013: xii[4]

This cultural stigmatization of disabled people has led to them being overlooked as consumers and producers by the fashion industry over time, resulting in very little documented evidence to study.

Another possible explanation is the intersection of disability and impoverished populations, who have generally been omitted from historical fashion analysis. Fashion as a construct was the domain of wealthy and privileged citizens well into the late nineteenth century, at which point it became "democratized," largely due to technological innovation and the birth of the ready-to-wear industry.[5] Museum collections tend to be replete with the possessions of wealthy and fashionable people who wore their items infrequently—in many cases only once—and could afford to prevent their degradation, if only through providing product-friendly storage conditions. Impoverished people lacked the resources to purchase new clothes, so items were worn until they disintegrated, or became more useful for other necessities. "New" garments for the poor were made over, or hand constructed from whatever fabric was available. It is unlikely that any clothing or textile items used by an economically disadvantaged disabled person would have survived, unless the wearer was part of a wealthy and fashionable socio-economic group and their clothing was customized to adapt by the family tailor, dressmaker or seamstress. Sunae Park Evans, Senior Costume Conservator at the Smithsonian Museum of American History, acknowledges that there are not many objects available for conservators and curators to study, and that she has rarely seen any objects related to accessibility and fashion during her tenure at the American History Museum, other than the sportswear associated with the Special Olympic Games and spotlighted in an exhibition hosted by the museum.[6]

A third explanation, and one which I find intriguing from a technical design perspective, is the lack of documentation and subsequent ambiguity surrounding fashion items in historic collections which have been altered, adapted, or otherwise edited to conform to a particular shape. Since many surviving garments that are housed in collections display obvious signs of manipulation, it is intriguing to wonder if changes in bodies were reasons for some of these adaptations, in addition to changes made to keep up with the latest trends. One must bear in mind that prior to the mid-nineteenth century, all clothing was custom made or handed on, and most items were altered, reshaped and otherwise edited to fit the wearer and/or the prevailing fashion silhouette of the time. The birth of ready-to-wear and the standardization of two-dimensional clothing patterns in the mid-nineteenth century led to a factory production system where pre-sized garments were manufactured in mass quantities. This in turn opened up fashion to the masses, but only if the masses' bodies conformed to pre-produced patterns and clothing shapes and sizing systems. The exhibit "Misfits: Bodies, Dress and Sustainability," staged by the University of Alberta in 2017, addressed this confusion in industrial sizing systems for clothing. Anne Bissonnette, lead curator of the exhibition, explained how the inclusion of bodies of disability in this exhibit was timely, stating that "We are ALL the people that fashion doesn't fit."[7] With these adaptations in mind, it is intriguing to think how much can be learned about the shapes of historical bodies from a reverse engineering approach by exploring fashion items in collections through measurement, comparison and analysis.

In carrying out research for this book, I discovered that historic collections do contain clothing items that have a documented history of having been altered to account for asymmetry of the body or other disability, both permanent and temporary. The ability of a disabled person with financial means to have garments tailored or adapted certainly continued after ready-to-wear restricted the fashion industry to a few-sizes-fit-all model, but only if they had access to the skills and other resources required. I also discovered that variations in bodies have long been acknowledged and accounted for in the tailoring trade. In the book *The London Tradesman* written by Campbell in 1747 as a description of contemporary trades, or as the preface states: "A Compendious View of all the Trades, Professions, Arts, both Liberal and Mechanic, now practised in the Cities of London and Westminster," language is included in the chapter titled "Tailor" to explain expectations and responsibilities in transforming bodies of fashion:

> He must be able, not only to cut for the Handsome and Well-shaped, but to bestow a good shape where Nature has not designed it; the Hump-back, the Wry-shoulder, must be buried in Flannel and Wadding, and the Coat must hang *de gage*, [at ease] though put over a Post: He must study not only the

Shape, but the common Gait of the Subject he is working upon, and make the Cloaths fit easy in spite of a stiff Gait, or awkard Air.

CAMPBELL 1747: 192[8]

An analysis of guidelines for tailors in the nineteenth century, which is discussed in ch. 3 of this book, shows how professional instruction manuals regularly included specific directions on patternmaking and stitching for bodies that differed significantly from the expected norms of the period. It is interesting that current technical textbooks lack similar resources for our modern students and trainees in higher education.

The research for this history relied both on primary and secondary sources. Extant examples of documented fashionable pieces that are positively identified as being designed and produced by and for disability prior to the 1930s are few, so I also reviewed contemporary texts and artwork such as paintings, illustrations, books and essays for evidence of the intersection between fashion and disability. There are some caveats in using secondary sources for historical research, which should be noted for transparency. For example, Andrews (2007) explains that clothing was portrayed in literature and art in England between 1650 and 1850 to differentiate "the insane" and also to appeal to society for charity, so some artistic records need to be viewed with this lens.[9] Public records provide some information but can be inconclusive. In the records of public asylums in Great Britain, for example, the way that institutions from the mid-seventeenth century onwards managed the appearance of physically disabled patients ranged from reports of complete nakedness, to the setting up of charitable clothing funds and drives, as well as charging patients for clothing by the piece. Generally, however, a description of the clothing itself is lacking, and certainly does not extend to any adaptations that were made to existing clothing for the benefit of the patients.

Medical texts and histories proved to be a valuable resource for some specific information about the continuing desire to reshape the "crooked" body, which was an especially important topic of conversation during the period of enlightenment and scientific discovery of the mid-eighteenth century. Authors of contemporary medical texts shared their thoughts and painstakingly-designed inventions directed at addressing physical "malformations" that were present in society, especially in children. These texts took the form of medical treatises, invention disclosures, and general advice directed at individuals, caregivers and parents. Although it is beyond the scope of this book to address purely medical textile products, which would now be referred to as assistive devices, the existence of this historic evidence underscores the prevalence of medical conditions giving rise to such devices, and the social reactions to these conditions. One could surmise that, due to the cost of some of these items, "correction" might have only been an option for the very wealthy in the eighteenth century.

I decided against inclusion of the Health Clothing Reform movement, which began during the Enlightenment but became a popular topic of public discussion and activism in the latter part of the nineteenth century. The reason for the avoidance is because this movement came about in reaction to perceived detrimental effects of mainstream fashion on women's health. It did not relate directly to disability but one could argue that it marked the first attempt at fashion gender equality, perhaps paving the way for other future shifts in fashion equality. The topic has also been covered in detail in other fashion history texts, references to which can be found at the end of this chapter for further investigation.[10] One of the prime targets of early campaigners for female equality—the corset—was an integral part of the fashionable silhouette for centuries, but it was also designed and sold as a spinal supporter and straightener, advocated as such by the medical community, and sold to women and men to help them achieve a "fashionable" silhouette. The corset, therefore, became an item to correct physical "deformities" but at the same time served to deform the body into artifice depending on the prevailing fashionable body profile.

Finally, the historic discussion will briefly include prosthetics. I consider a prosthetic, broadly defined, to be a modern part of the contemporary fashion lexicon, providing a means for people to construct and crystallize their identity and self-expression. Additionally, fashion may have shaped the way prosthetics were designed throughout history. Vittorio Putti (1930), in the book *Historic Artificial Limbs*, stated:

> It is supposed that a maimed fellow would try to find a remedy for his imperfections ... the art of making artificial limbs has greatly improved

since the revival of surgery during the 15th and 16th centuries, when the technic [sic] of amputations was submitted to more systematic rules and surgeons took more interest in the construction of such artificial contrivances, advising and directing the artisan in his work.

PUTTI, 1930: vii[11]

This comment suggests medical input in the artistic making of limbs, with surgeons acting as both medical advisors and creative directors. We will see this idea echoed somewhat in reverse in conversations with contemporary fashion designers in ch. 6, where there is much discussion about fashion designers needing to embed themselves on a deeper collaborative level with medical practice in order to have a clear understanding of the consumer of adaptive fashion. I will briefly cover how artificial limbs from the sixteenth century onwards charted a course for decorative and fashionable elements, which are echoed in contemporary design initiatives such as the Alternative Limb Project.[12]

I have been mindful of the use of the term "fashion" as it has been set up in ch. 1, so for research purposes I have operationalized the term to mean clothing and accessories. This still creates complexity, because fashion AND disability as linguistic terms tend to have multiple "homes" in museum and library collections and archival documentation. Much care was taken in setting up appropriate search terms once I decided to expand to the product (clothing/accessories) in addition to the concept (fashion). In addition, I write with the assumption that readers have some knowledge of basic Western fashion history—if not I strongly recommend the Fashion History Timeline, produced by the Fashion Institute of Technology (FIT).[13] A summary timeline graphic for this newly-constructed Disability Fashion History will be found at the end of this book.

2.2 Pre-Eighteenth Century

This story of the intersection between fashion and disability begins in the mid-sixteenth century, even though disability had been part of daily life for hundreds of years prior to this era. Penrose, writing about disability in Ancient Greece argued that: "the political, social, medical, institutional, and cultural climates in ancient Greek societies varied from our own, but a contrast between the able-bodied and disabled was socially constructed in ancient Greece."[14] (Penrose 2015: 504) Multiple types of disabling conditions are also apparent as a result of tomb excavations in Ancient Egypt.[15] Artists in Ancient Rome depicted disabled people with greater frequency than other ancient cultures, in mosaics, statuary, wall paintings, and accessories.[16] Jane Draycott, in the book *Prostheses in Antiquity*, discusses how wealthy Greeks had prostheses that were "cosmetic rather than functional" and that they had the ability "to requisition the labour of others." (Draycott 2019: 9).[17]

However, any details about the knowledge with which fashionable people were able to address differences in body types through their clothing prior to the Renaissance has not been well documented or researched. This book therefore begins its historical journey in the mid-sixteenth century with the invention of a crude iron corset, developed by the royal French surgeon, Ambroise Paré, who invented this device to "straighten" the torso of his patients. The title of the image depicting the device (Fig. 2.1), taken from "The Works of

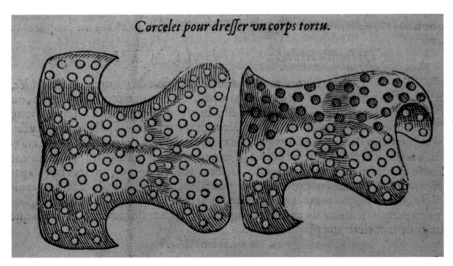

Figure 2.1 *Ambroise Paré's invention of an iron corset. Image shows the front and back of a corset structure for the upper body, with holes punched throughout both pieces. From Chapter VIII, p.951, Les Ouvres d'Ambroise Paré (4th edition), published by Gabriel Buon, Paris, 1585*

Ambroise Paré," literally translates to "Corcelet to train a twisted body." (Buon 1585: 951)[18] The later English translation of Buon's book, published in 1634 by Thomas Johnson, describes the device as "The forme of an iron Breast-plate, to amend the crookednesse of the Body." (Johnson 1634: 876).[19]

Johnson's English translation of Paré's purpose for the invention reads as follows:

> Of amending the deformity of such as are crooke-backt. The bodies of many, especially young maids or girles . . . are made crooked in processe of time, especially by the wrenching aside and crookednesse of the backe-bone. It hath many causes . . . in the wombe, and afterwards by misfortune, as a fall, bruise, or any such like accident, but especially by the unhandsome and undecent situation of their bodies, when they are young and tender . . . . crookednesse, that happens seldome to the country people, but is much incident to the inhabitants of great townes and cities, which is by reason of the straitnesse and narrownesse of the garments that are worne by them, which is occasioned by the folly of mothers, who while they covet to have their young daughters bodies so small in the middle as may be possible, plucke and draw their bones awry, and make them crooked . . . The remedy for this deformity is to have breast-plates of iron, full of holes all over them, wherby they may be lighter to wear; and they must be so lined with bombast [cotton padding], that they may hurt no place of the body. Every three moneths new plates must be made for those that are not yet arrived at their full growth . . . But these plates will do them small good that are already at their full growth.
>
> JOHNSON 1634: 876

Much can be learned from this and other examples of Paré's work and also from his written observations. It is clear from Paré's opinions of sixteenth-century ladies' fashion, which apparently necessitated young girls to have tiny waists, thus modifying bone growth and placement, that he realized that fashionable practices were dangerous for women's bodies. Not only that, but in his "cure" of an iron breastplate lightened through perforations and changed out every three months to accommodate natural growth patterns, we witness a medical practitioner commenting on and providing solutions for the "disabling" (urban) fashions of his time. This sets the stage for future iterations of the corset leading a double-life as both orthopedic device and fashionable body-shaper. According to Steele (2001): "by the seventeenth century, girls as young as two years wore miniature corsets to support the body."[20] This suggests a chicken and egg question at this point—did the corset destroy or provide salvation for the female body, and which came first? No doubt the causes are complex and much more ancient than we have space to examine here, but we witness with Paré's addressing of the issue one of the first points of documented intersectionality between fashion and disability.

It is also worth mentioning that Ambroise Paré was prolific in his inventions of artificial limbs and body parts during his career as a surgeon. Vittorio Putti in his book on *Historic Artificial Limbs* (1930) mentions that many early prosthetic hands and legs were the result of the French surgeon's inventions, used by soldiers to conceal injuries sustained during military conflict. It is interesting to note that decorative elements were applied to assistive devices from the sixteenth century onwards for fashionable men who could afford it.

Torso and spinal "deformities" were not the only physical issues addressed through wearable products during the Renaissance. The fashion of the early to mid-sixteenth century for slashed shoes (see Fig. 2.2), in some instances may have been adapted for the purposes of accommodating feet with bunions or gout (an extreme form of arthritis). During the Renaissance, slashing was a fashionable technique used not only on shoes, but also in clothing, however the origins are debatable. It is therefore difficult to determine which shoes might have been slashed for medical rather than fashionable purposes. Some researchers have commented that slits were cut into the vamp of the shoe to relieve bunion joints. D.A. Saguto, former master shoemaker at Colonial Williamsburg, (restored colonial capital of Virginia and important living history museum in the US), states: "From looking at the shoes that survive, you can easily deduce the pathology of the foot . . . you can see all the same problems orthopedic shoemakers see today . . . Archeologists have dug up leather footwear from the Middle Ages, the uppers of which had been slashed to accommodate bunions and hammertoes."[21] Saguto also mentions that the first orthopedic shoemakers were French, based in Paris, but the industry started about one hundred years after Paré's work on orthopedic corsets began. Like

Figure 2.2 *Leather slip-on shoe with evenly-spaced slashed decoration near the toe; representative of many found during the 1988–91 excavations at the Rose and Globe playhouses in London. Photo by MOLA/Getty Images*

the corset, this historical data about shoes leads to consideration of how fashionable embellishment may have doubled as functional adaptation. It is worth mentioning here that King Henry VIII of England, whose portraits show him wearing slashed shoes—a fashionable departure from the extremely pointed shoes that had been popular prior to his reign—suffered from severe gout.

Some of the first existing physical evidence of adaptation of clothing can be found in the seventeenth-century closets of the very fashionable and wealthy. In the collection of Claydon House, a National Trust property in Buckinghamshire, England, there are two men's suits dated between 1660–62, which are not only rare examples of complete doublet and breeches combinations from this period (Lesley Edwards states that these are the only surviving full suits from this period), but evidence suggests that they were also adapted to address the severe body asymmetry of the wearer.[22] Indications are that they belonged to Edmund "Mun" Verney, an aristocrat with royal connections—his grandfather had been Knight-Marshal and Standard Bearer to King Charles I. Mun grew up with a congenital spinal condition, and was subjected to "cures" during his youth involving the wearing of a leather-lined iron harness, under which a linen shirt was worn to absorb perspiration and provide some comfort. Edwards explains, "The shirt was changed once a week by which time it was 'as black as a chimney." (Edwards 1985: 75) Edwards suggests, after much research using the adapted garments, that Mun's condition was scoliosis—a twisted spine and "shoulders out of alignment". (ibid: 76)

When he was twenty years old, Verney was fitted with special "bodies" (a type of corset) at great cost, to "disguise" his condition. In addition to undergarments, some external aspects of fashions of the day may have also helped to "disguise" his physical condition. In a painting in the collection at Claydon House commissioned to mark his twenty-first birthday, Mun's cloak is draped over his left shoulder. It is possible that artistic convention might have dictated the wearing of the cloak, but it could also have been used to cover up his asymmetry. Internally, the two doublets (jackets) both have extensive padding covering the back neck, shoulder and armhole to the center back seam on one side. The padding varies in thickness and consists of layers of black wool felt stitched together. There is no doubt from the external aspect of his clothing that Mun was a man of fashion. The suits are trimmed with lengths of decorative ribbon, which was very much the fashion of the second half of the seventeenth century. Edwards states: "the ribbons on the surviving suits show that Edmund eventually acquired a lavishly beribboned suit" (Edwards 1985: 85). Edwards makes an interesting point regarding the miraculous survival of these two suits: "The suits were made for a person with a disability and would not have comfortably fitted another person without restructuring the doublets ... They may have survived *because* they were unusual" (Edwards 1985: 92). For the reader familiar with preservation of historic costume, the "making-over" of garments into newer fashions is a familiar practice. However, Mun's suits seem to have remain untouched, making Edwards' observations all the more intriguing.

Lesley Edwards (1983) is also responsible for research and documentation regarding a long-sleeved waistcoat which has been dated to 1720–30 in the collection of the Gallery of English Costume in Platt Hall, Manchester, England (see Figs 2.3, 2.4, 2.5).[23] Edwards suggests that the waistcoat in the Manchester collection has been adapted to fit a person with scoliosis. Edwards consulted with tailors in Savile Row, London, during her research and suggests that interior padding on one side of the coat could: "have been added to compensate for a hollow of some form". (Edwards 1983: 62).

Figure 2.3 *Platt Hall waistcoat, 1720–30, showing front and pockets flaps decorated with embroidered floral motifs. Courtesy of the Gallery of Costume, Manchester Art Gallery*

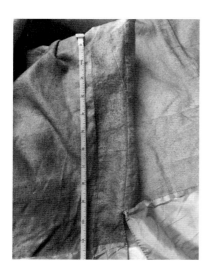

Figure 2.4 *Platt Hall waistcoat—interior view showing insertion of fabric strip to widen the coat on one side Courtesy of the Gallery of Costume, Manchester Art Gallery*

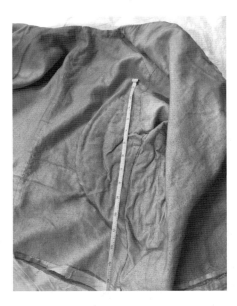

Figure 2.5 *Platt Hall waistcoat—interior view showing padding under wearer's left arm. Courtesy of the Gallery of Costume, Manchester Art Gallery*

Around the same time, adaptations were also being made at the fashionable royal court in England, but in response to a disability created as the result of an accident. In early March 1702, King William III was thrown from his horse while riding in a park in London. He broke his collarbone in the fall and was fitted with a splint to wear as treatment to assist the bones to heal, rendering the clothing almost impossible to don and doff (put on and take off) on that side of his body. To accommodate the splint and allow the King's servants to dress him, one of his garments, a sleeved waistcoat, was opened up on top of the right sleeve and ties were stitched into place along the shoulder seam and along the opening so that bows could be tied to fasten the sleeve. Fig. 2.6 shows a sleeved waistcoat with these ties belonging to King William in the collection of the Rijksmuseum in the Netherlands. The adaptation allowed the garment to be wrapped around the arm and shoulder areas and over the splint, without having to move the arm and cause further discomfort. The bows in this example appear hastily made and cut from fabric without the edges being finished, and the cut seams have been rapidly finished with a running stitch (see Fig. 2.7). However, the overall external effect is quite similar to the fashionable men's garments of the late seventeenth century, as evidenced in the

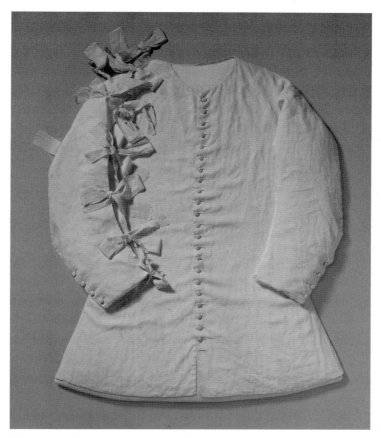

Figure 2.6 *Sleeved waistcoat with bows, worn by King William III of England, made prior to 1702. Image shows a white sleeved waistcoat with buttons up the front and the top of the wearer's right sleeve tied together with bows of white fabric. Courtesy Rijksmuseum, Amsterdam*

suits at Claydon Hall, "bedecked" with their fashionable ribbons tied into bows. Whether fashion had anything to do with the functional adaptation of the King's vest is unknown—since the bows were not replicated on the other sleeve the effect may not have been intentional. But could it be possible that the King's surgeons and tailors were influenced by contemporary fashion as they were figuring out a way to hastily adapt this waistcoat to assist in treatment of his injury?

Figure 2.7 *Detail of sleeved waistcoat with bows, worn by King William III of England, made prior to 1702. Image shows a close-up of sleeve edge and ties. Courtesy Rijksmuseum, Amsterdam*

Turning our attention across the Atlantic, it seems appropriate to begin the narrative of fashion and disability in North America with its indigenous peoples. Native Americans had a holistic approach to disabled bodies. They believed that the entirety of any organism is important and that everything and everyone has a gift to offer. Kim Nielsen (2013) writes of pre-Columbian societies; "The daily life of someone who was deaf, blind, moved with the rhythms of cerebral palsy, or who could not walk or had difficulty walking, is hard to discern for the centuries prior to European arrival in North America . . . It is likely that being disabled had little impact on the measurement of an individual's capacity" (Nielsen 2013: 6).[24] How does this attitude translate into the types of garments and accessories worn and carried by Native Americans? We know that native people wore "binary garments—best described as two pieces of material about the same shape and size, which covered the front and back body, and which were either stitched or tied on the sides" (Blanco 2015: 192).[25] Other clothing was constructed by wrapping and folding materials around the body and somehow tied or belted. This way of clothing the body was roomy, unfitted and could be draped over virtually any body type. Looking at the paintings by Alexandre de Batz (Fig. 2.8), who in 1735 created the earliest known views of Native Americans in the lower Mississippi Valley, one can see the geometric material shapes used for body

Figure 2.8 *Desseins de Sauvages de Plusieurs Nations, Alexandre de Batz, 1735. Image shows people along the banks of a river wearing skirts, decorative loincloths and body paint. Gift of the Estate of Belle J. Bushnell, 1941. Courtesy the Peabody Museum of Archaeology and Ethnology, Harvard University, 41-72-10/20*

coverage by men, women and children, which would have been easily adaptable to a variety of body types.

The same is true for de Batz's sketches of indigenous peoples in winter clothing, showing how clothing used for warmth was equally accessible for easy body coverage, no matter the body shape, due to the simple geometric shape of the clothing items, suitable for wrapping around the body. Is it coincidental that, lacking a cultural attitude of otherness towards disabled people, the clothing of indigenous peoples in North America naturally accommodated all body types and abilities through its geometric simplicity and ability for wearer adaptation and self-fashioning?

As European settlers arrived on American eastern shores in the seventeenth and eighteenth centuries, colonial communities established guidelines for those who could not participate in cultural life due to physical and/or cognitive limitations. For the most part, communities in Colonial America expected families to provide for their disabled family members. If caring for a disabled family member was impossible for socio-economic reasons, the disabled person became the responsibility of the community. From the beginnings of immigration to the American colonies, however, laws had been passed to discourage disabled people from even entering. In these early laws, to be a disabled person was seen as being unable to maintain oneself economically. Almshouses, poor-houses, and workhouses were set up as early as the early 1700s to house disabled poor people who were descendants of established settlers. Since there are written accounts of wealthy early settlers whose family members had a disability, due to accident, birth or disease, it can be assumed that steps were taken to find ways to clothe and manage the appearance of the family member. We know that these wealthy early settlers were concerned with Eurocentric fashionable life, yet little evidence exists of how they navigated fashionable clothing and accessories for disabled family members.[26]

Little is known about slavery, disability, and fashion in the American colonies and in other parts of the world that benefited from the slave trade during this time period. Any communication that people who were held in captivity and were owned by other human beings would be part of fashionable life has not figured into early colonial accounts of enslaved people's lives. Clothing, or lack of it, had been used to subjugate enslaved people, first by the perpetrators of the slave trade to reduce captive people to comparison with animals, and in later years of enslavement, when clothing was very much a part of the identification and recapture process when enslaved people were trying to escape to freedom. Hunt-Kennedy (2020: 104) explains how clothing was used as the "key distinguishing factor, not the individual's body."[27] Slaveowners provided enslaved people with clothing, and for some, this was done with fashionable clothing "as a sign of their [slaveowners] prestige and wealth." (Hunt-Kennedy 2020: 104). We do have evidence of disability in the colonial enslaved population: "Blindness also made regular appearances in runaway advertisements, though the condition did not necessarily impair one's ability to be productive on the plantation, where it was more common for bondspeople to experience a loss of vision due to environmental conditions." (Hunt-Kennedy 2020: 117). There was also evidence that clothing was used to *conceal* disfigurements and disability of enslaved people trying to escape to freedom to render them less conspicuous.

2.3 Impact of the Age of Enlightenment: 1740–1800[28]

As the American Colonies negotiated their way through independence in the eighteenth century, Europe was becoming rife with inventions of devices for correcting bodies that did not fit in with the fashionable ideal. For example, the theme and treatment of spinal asymmetry was the subject of medical monographs and essays, demonstrating an interest in moving beyond the simple corset to a more dramatic means of body correction. French medical doctor Levacher de la Feutrie (1772) illustrated and explained inventions to "correct" body types through therapeutic devices, mainly for children.[29] One option showed a system of iron corsetry coupled with an iron brace, which was attached to the head, neck and spine (Fig. 2.9). Although not "fashionable" dress, the presence of devices such as this shows a concern for "'straightness" of the body and indication of the existence of spinal inconsistencies in children during this period. Since treatments such as this would no doubt have been costly, one can infer that the problem of "crookedness" was prevalent enough among wealthy and fashionable families to elicit inventions such as this one, so that children would grow up with the required fashionably straight posture.

Turner and Withey (2014: 777) explain how "studying the development of devices aimed to correct or conceal [physical attributes deemed] 'deformities' provides a unique insight into the convergence of technological progress and cultural values in eighteenth-century England".[30] These devices "fashioned" the body for cultural value by utilizing new materials, such as cast steel, an invention of the 1770s, which possessed the property of "tensile, springy strength" as well as aesthetic appeal (cast steel became so popular that it was made into jewelry due to its highly polished effect). The new material encouraged and supported entrepreneurial growth in the industry of "corrective" devices, which made their way back and forth across the Atlantic. Truss-making (trusses were worn to support hernias); back irons (worn concealed under fashionable clothes to promote a straight spine) and steel collars (worn to "uphold the chin") were among the popular corrective and assistive devices through which we can discern the eighteenth-century fashionable society's cultural obsession with straightness.

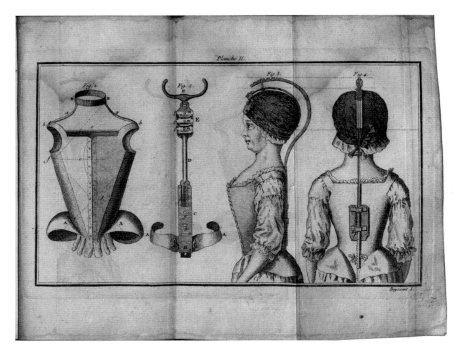

Figure 2.9 *Apparatus for treatment of rickets in children, by Levacher de la Feutrie, 1772. Image shows a metal corset and back brace, both off and on a person, side and back views. Courtesy David M. Rubenstein Rare Book & Manuscript Library, Duke University*

Another condition receiving much attention in medical texts during the eighteenth century was palsy, a type of paralysis accompanied by uncontrolled shaking of the body.[31] In 1791 an opinion piece written by a medical doctor encouraged the use of "fleecy hosiery" (made from wool) to alleviate the conditions brought on by palsy.[32] In the doctor's opinion, since fleece (wool) worked well for animals that it came from, it should also work well for humans, since above all other fabrics, wool: ". . . affords the greatest warmth with the least weight." (Buchan 1791: 8). There is also mention of its hygienic properties and that it is "free from smells, washes with ease and is less apt to harbour vermin." (Buchan 1791: 9). Hosiery was believed to be the best garment to help this condition because it "increases friction against the skin and promotes discharge, which is carried off by the conducting power of the wool." (Buchan 1791: 9).

The medical community was obviously leveraging some of wool fiber's finest attributes—its ability to absorb and to conduct moisture. The letter goes on to explain how Sir Benjamin Thomson's experiments at the Royal Society in London demonstrated how woolen clothes promoted "insensible perspiration," (Buchan 1791: 12) and "favours its evaporation," (Buchan 1791: 13). The letter discussed the benefits of woolen garments worn next to the skin, to alleviate the effects of variable weather conditions: "The torpor of a paralytic limb renders some warm and stimulating application necessary; and this intention is more likely to be answered by your hosiery than by flannel, as it not only possesses a greater degree of warmth, but is, from its texture, better adapted to act as a stimulus to the skin." (Buchan 1791: 26) When one considers that today's hosiery industry includes robust product lines in support and medical hose, the similarities with perceived eighteenth-century benefits of "fleecy" hosiery for short- and long-term use to promote circulation in the lower limbs, become apparent.

The eighteenth century also provides us with an early English commentary on being a disabled person in full view of society, written by a man of wealth and public status. William Hay, Esq. penned *Deformity: An Essay*, published in 1754.[33] Hay was a well-respected Member of Parliament (MP) for the county of Sussex in England. He was elected to Parliament in 1734 and remained in public service until his death in 1755. He is said to have been dedicated to his work, as well as being a strong advocate for the poor and contributor to the development of the silk industry in the Spitalfields area of London. Hay was five feet in height, hunchbacked, and visually impaired due to a childhood case of smallpox. Hay's essay "offers a unique glimpse into the lived experience of a person with a disability in enlightenment London" (James-Cavan 2004: 10). Hay speaks of fashion just once in his essay, but his opinion is clear when he states:

> Fine Cloaths attract the Eyes of the Vulgar: and therefore a deformed Person would not assume those borrowed Feathers, which will render him doubly ridiculous ... Ever since I have arrived at Years of Discretion, I have worn a plain Dress; which, for near thirty years, has been of the same grave Colour; and which I find not the least inclination to alter. It would be monstrous in me to bestow any Ornament on a Person, which is incapable of it; and should I appear in Lace or Embroidery, my Friends might assign it as no unreasonable Pretence for a Commission or Lunacy against me.
>
> JAMES-CAVAN 2004: 41

Hay's words provide evidence that he considered fashionable clothes ("borrowed Feathers") to be inappropriate for him to wear because he felt that his disabilities could not support the ornamentation. He evidently felt that it would be ridiculous for him to participate in a world of fashion due to his appearance. Similar undertones exist today regarding age and disability and assumptions about whether disabled people and some other populations are included in a fashionable world.

Twigg (2013) discusses such assumptions about clothing for older people in the book *Fashion and Age*.[34] Twigg explores the intersections between aging and fashion, and the tension of engagement of age with an aesthetic designed to be targeted at a youthful, energetic society. Twigg goes on to observe a return to childishness in some clothing designed for the very old: "the dress of the very young and the very old is similar in terms of materials, colours and fastenings, with bright pale colours, easy-clean fabrics and elastic cut" (Twigg 2013: 13). These observations echo the frustration of disabled consumers in conversations that I have had during research projects. Many disabled people talk about the prevalence of elastic and/or Velcro fastenings, easy-clean but unexciting and unappealing fabrics, and in the retail environment, assistants who ask questions of their abled friends as if they (the customer) are unable to speak for themselves.

Women interviewed for Twigg's research reflect some of William Hay's attitude towards fashion in the twenty-first century. These women had mixed feelings about fashion, but they all noticed that norms around age-related fashion issues had "continuing power" (Twigg 2013: 73):

> Some of the negative comments expressed in the interviews about the body and appearance, with their preemptive quality, reflected such a response. Adopting toned-down, dull forms of dress could be a means of hiding, or not drawing attention to the self. Strong colours, bold patterns and fashionable styles threatened the reverse, consciously drawing the eye and making a claim to attention.
>
> TWIGG 2013: 63

Reading Hay's essay certainly invites parallels between the fears of older modern women, not wanting to claim attention, and Hay's eighteenth-century opinion that "Fine Cloaths attract the Eyes of the Vulgar." Apparently Hay experienced societal pressures to "fit in," even from his friends, curtailing any desire to dress in the latest fashions.

Continuing on the historical journey, and returning to the American colonies, evidence suggests that by the eighteenth century colonists were as adept as their European counterparts in altering existing products or designing new ones when they needed better solutions for disability needs. Belolan (2020: 20) explains that most material needs for people with physical disabilities were satisfied through improvisation "in collaboration with friends, family, craftspeople, servants and enslaved people using whatever resources they had at hand."[35] Some of these forms of improvisation should certainly be considered early assistive devices. People who were part of fashionable society may have had the same physical disabilities as the poor, but social and cultural life would have required them to maintain a face of public display. As an example, fashionable men were still wearing breeches to just below the knee and stockings over their calves and feet. The male calf was considered an attribute, but gout tended to affect the lower limbs, so the wealthy would "hide their gout . . . with a soft blanket made and marketed specifically . . . but the working poor had fewer means to hide it." (Belolan 2020: 27) The use of "fleecy hosiery," previously mentioned for treating the symptoms of palsy, was also popular to hide "disfiguring lumps and bumps," and also to encourage sweating, which was thought to rid the body of disease. Gout also led to the development of adapted shoes, accommodating changes and swelling in the feet. These adaptations were similar to how shoes may have been "slashed" in the sixteenth century to alleviate bunions and other issues. Belolan explains that in 1789 in the newly-formed United States, Pennsylvania Surveyor General John Lukens, a man of "wealth and station" (Belolan 2020: 19), ordered a four-wheeled pleasure carriage to accommodate his chronic case of gout. The knowledge that the fashionably wealthy redesigned furniture and vehicles invites the assumption that they might also have redesigned their clothing to accommodate their disabilities.

Summary

Despite little obvious documentation of historical evidence relating disability to fashionable life prior to 1800, this chapter sheds light on some pieces of evidence that demonstrate (a) people of fashion were also disabled people, and (b) attempts were being made by tailors, dressmakers, and medical practitioners to creatively adapt clothing to fit the needs of people with long- and short-term disabilities. In addition, the preoccupation of creating devices to straighten torsos and spines that were out of alignment shows a Western fascination with an ideal of a fashionable body as having a ramrod straight posture.

Fashionable clothing, which was adapted by ingenious tailors for Mun Verney, King William III and the owner of the Platt Hall waistcoat show that the tailor's goal was to do everything possible within his skill to enable his customer to live a life of fashion through clothing. We see evidence of clothing being padded out, having pieces inserted, sliced up, and adapted with alternative fastenings. This begins to beg the question of whether every tailor and couturier who makes a custom item of clothing is "adapting" it to the body to a certain extent? Not one body is symmetrical or shaped exactly like another, therefore the act of tailoring is always going to involve the act of adaptation from a standard. Tailors, at least, were trained and expected to fit the fashionable body no matter how as much it departed from the "norm."

We also have a first-hand account of what it was like to live a fashionable life in a disabled body in the eighteenth century. William Hay speaks of dressing plainly, and that he would find it ridiculous to be wearing any type of ornamented or fashionable clothing which would draw attention to his disability, perhaps an indicator of cultural attitudes towards disability in London at the time as much as his own attitudes.

In terms of early American colonial life, there is little to be assessed at this point, given the lack of evidence in primary and secondary sources. It is hoped that more work can be done in this area, however, we do know that fashion as a concept was imported from Western Europe for early settlers in the colonies. There is also some evidence that enslaved people might have been given fashionable clothing to wear by their owners, but there is little documented evidence of how this might have intersected with disability.

Profiles: Mrs. Morrell and Miss Hawtin

Each historic period included in this book includes a profile of a figure who represents in some way the intersection of fashion with disability. For this chapter, I have chosen to focus on two women who lived in the eighteenth century and shared the same disability—Mrs. Mary Morrell and Miss Hawtin, both from England, who were born without arms.

The British Museum has in its collection a portrait of Miss Hawtin, from Coventry, Warwickshire, from 1774, which shows her sitting on a table cutting watch papers, holding a paper with her right foot and cutting the paper with scissors held in the toes of her left foot. Little is known about how she adapted clothing to fit her body type, but she is dressed in a fashionable gown with short sleeves, and she has decorative flowers in her hair. Her appearance is in line with the fashions of the time. The Norfolk Chronicle, dated October 30, 1784, in a notice advertising that Miss Hawtin will be "exhibited" from 2:00 p.m. until 9:00 p.m. at the Crown in Canterbury, explains: "She threads a needle, sews, picks pins or needles out of a pin-cushion, and sticks them in again; uses the scissors dexterously, in cutting out devices in paper. . ."

Another Englishwoman whose portrait appears in the British Museum collections was Mrs. Mary Morrell. Mrs. Morrell was depicted in a print by Robert Thew, historical engraver to His Majesty Prince of Wales, dated between 1778 and 1802 (Fig. 2.10). She

Figure 2.10 *Portrait of Mrs. Morell, print made by Robert Thew, production date 1778–1802. Paper, stipple etching. Image shows a woman without arms in fashionable dress, holding a pair of scissors in toes of her left foot. A set of papers are lying next to her right foot. Courtesy Department of Prints and Drawings in the British Museum © The Trustees of the British Museum, Registration number 1851,0308.453*

is shown seated with her feet coming out from under her skirt and apron and is dressed in fashionable Georgian clothing of the late eighteenth century, with a built-up hairstyle, curls, and bonnet, a crossover apron with embroidered edging, and a gown that has no indication of any armholes. Unfortunately it is impossible to tell whether artistic convention did not allow alterations to the gown to be depicted, or if this was a garment that was designed and stitched specifically for the wearer. In any case, it is interesting to see some suggestion of adaptation, because when other people are shown without arms, the sleeves are generally still attached to a garment but somehow shortened or tied up. This garment, according to the print, does not give obvious visual indication that it ever had sleeves, unless they are tucked away inside the apron.

The print shows her cutting watch-paper like Miss Hawtin. She is depicted holding a small pair of scissors in her left toes and with a thimble on her big right toe, with a small book to her right side. Mrs. Morrell was apparently quite well known and exhibited to the public in a similar way to Miss Hawtin. An excerpt from the Manchester Mercury, June 10, 1794, explains: "Born without arms, and will work with her toes, in a complete manner as with hands and arms, she cuts watch papers, opens watches and puts the papers in. This curious artist threads her needle well and does wonder of the age excel! She, with her TOES, exhibits more to view than thousands, with their fingers, ev'r can do . . ."

Notes

1   MetMuseum.org. (2011), "661,509 Total Visitors to Alexander McQueen Put Retrospective among Top 10 Most Visited Exhibitions in Metropolitan Museum's History", *Met Museum Press*, August 8th. Available online: https://www.metmuseum. org/press/news/2011/mcqueen-attendance (accessed February 24, 2020).

2   Hollander, S. (2011), "Not Since the 'Mona Lisa'.*" The Wall Street Journal*, August 6. Available online: https://www.wsj.com/articles/SB1000142405311190345450457649070 0643776500 (accessed March 2, 2021).

3   Anne Bissonnette, personal conversation, February 9, 2021.

4   Nielsen, K. (2013), *A Disability History of the United States*, Boston: Beacon Press.

5   Kidwell, C.B. and Christman, M.C. (1974), *Suiting Everyone: The Democratization of Clothing in America*, Washington, DC: Smithsonian Institution Press, provides a deep insight into this process.

6   Sunae Park Evans, personal conversation, May 18, 2020. The Special Olympics exhibit mentioned was the *Special Olympics at 50* online exhibition, which closed October 2021.

7   Anne Bissonnette, personal conversation, February 9, 2021.

8   Campbell, R. (1747), *The London Tradesman*, originally published by T. Gardner, London in 1747. Reprinted by Augustus M. Kelley, Publishers, New York, 1969.

9   Andrews, J. (2007), "The (un)dress of the mad poor in England, c.1650–1850: Part 2", *History of Psychiatry*, 18(2): 5–24.

10 Newton, S.M. (1974), *Health, Art and Reason: Dress reformers of the 19th century*. London: J. Murray; Sprinthall, C. (1986), Nineteenth century dress reform: changing the shape of women's lives, thesis, Duke University; the writings of Abba Goold Woolson, lectures on the Dress Reform movement in the US, can be used to find information on the Dress Reform movement.

11 Putti, V. (1930), *Historic Artificial Limbs*, Paul B. Hoeber, Inc: New York.

12 Alternative Limb Project, (2022). Available online: https://thealternativelimbproject.com/ (accessed December 22, 2022).

13 FIT State University of New York, (2022), Fashion History Timeline. Available online: https://fashionhistory.fitnyc.edu/ (accessed December 22, 2022).

14 Penrose, W.D., Jr. (2015), "The Discourse of Disability in Ancient Greece", *Classical World*, 108 (4): 499–523.

15 David, R. (2017), "Egyptian Medicine and Disabilities: From pharaonic to Greco-Roman Egypt", in *Disability in Antiquity*, C. Laes (ed.), Oxford: Routledge.

16 Trentin, L. (2017), "The 'Other' Romans: Deformed bodies in the visual arts of Rome", in *Disability in Antiquity*, C. Laes (Ed), Oxford: Routledge.

17 Draycott, J. (2019), (ed.), *Prostheses in Antiquity*, London: Routledge.

18 Buon, G. (1585), *The Works of Ambroise Paré*. Paris.

19 Johnson, T. (1634), *The Collected Works of Ambroise Paré, translated out of the Latin by Thomas Johnson*, Pound Ridge, NY: Milford House, 1968.

20 Steele, V. (2001), *The Corset: A Cultural History*, New Haven and London: Yale University Press, 12.

21 Craig, B. (2006), "If the Shoe Fits, It Might Be Made the 18th Century Way", *O&P Business News*, February 1, 2006, 51–3.

22 Edwards, L. (1985), "Dres't like a May-Pole", *Costume: The Journal of the Costume Society*, 19: 75–93.

23 Edwards, L. (1983), "Retrospective diagnosis of an eighteenth-century waistcoat", *Costume: The Journal of the Costume Society*, 17: 59–63.

24 Nielsen, K. (2013), *A Disability History of the United States*, Boston: Beacon Press.

25 Blanco, J. (ed.), (2015), *Clothing and Fashion: American Fashion from Head to Toe*, [4 Volumes], United States: ABC-CLIO.

26 According to Blanco et al., clothing of settlers reflected the cultural background that they had left in Europe. Since there were many nationalities leaving Europe and settling in the colonies, these fashions were as varied as the settlers themselves.

27 Hunt-Kennedy, S. (2020), *Between fitness and death: Disability and Slavery in the Caribbean*, Champaign: University of Illinois Press.

28 The Age of Enlightenment, or Age of Reason, which is characterized by some scholars as the beginning of the Modern Age, is defined by significant changes in science, philosophy, politics, and industry throughout the Western world. The period spanned roughly the entire eighteenth century.

29 The full title of the book translates to "Treatment of Rickets, or the art of straightening malformed children." Levacher de la Feutrie, T. (1772), *"Traité du rakitis, ou, l'art de redresser les enfants contrefaits"*, Paris.

30 Turner, D.M. and Withey, A. (2014), "Technologies of the body: Polite Consumption and the Correction of Deformity in Eighteenth Century England", *History: The Journal of the Historical Association*, 99 (338): 775–96.

31 MedicalDictionary (2021), *"Palsy"*. Available online: https://medical-dictionary. thefreedictionary.com/palsy (accessed April 6, 2021).

32 Buchan, W. (1791), *"A letter to the patentee [G. Holland] concerning the medical properties of the fleecy hosiery"*, by William Buchan, London, from Peterborough-House press, by D and D. Stuart, 1791. 4th edn, with additional notes and observations by the editor.

33 Hay, W. (1754), *Deformity: An Essay*, Ed. Kathleen James-Cavan. English Literary Series. Victoria BC: University of Victoria, 2004. Print.

34 Twigg, J. (2013), *Fashion and Age: Dress, the Body and Later Life*, London: Bloomsbury Academic.

35 Belolan, N. (2020), "The Material Culture of Gout in Early America", in *Making Disability Modern: Design Histories*, B. Williamson and E. Guffey (eds), London: Bloomsbury.

3

Improvisation and Innovation: 1800–1920

Introduction

This chapter focuses on the nineteenth century through to the end of the First World War, and includes stories of notable figures from this period whose fashionable lives intersected with their identity as disabled people, either through acquired disabling conditions, or a condition from birth. One goal of this chapter is to show how adaptations and improvisations were made to fashionable clothing, which in the case of one military leader, became a design option for subsequent generations of fashion designers. Another goal is to examine the fashionable expectations of physicality and the entrepreneurial drive to supply items that made bodies appear "normal" to society, such as "orthopedic" corsets and "natural-looking" prosthetics. The chapter also covers how adaptations existed in the clothing of the highest social classes, including royalty, in an effort to conceal aspects of physical bodies that could not be revealed to the fashionable public. Finally, there is a short explanation of how public opinion and policy towards managed care of disabled people started to change from institutionalization to rehabilitation at the beginning of the twentieth century due to the effects of the First World War and the polio epidemic in the United States.

3.1 The Early to Mid-Nineteenth Century

By the beginning of the nineteenth century, Western fashion followed a prescriptive pattern that originated for the most part in the royal courts and aristocratic social circles of Europe (primarily France and England), then made its way across the Atlantic to North America and to various other parts of the colonized world. Being part of this hierarchical system was exclusionary and inevitably confined to the wealthy, the privileged and those whose lives were entwined with fashionable social circles.

At the turn of the eighteenth century, it was well known that the English monarch, George III, was suffering from a form of psychiatric disability. Most sources attribute his episodic presentations of illness to a hereditary condition, but recent research has shed new light on his condition and multiple chronic symptoms. Peters and Wilkinson (2010: 5) mention that the King suffered from physically violent outbursts which were treated "by the use of a 'straight waistcoat'" prescribed by his doctor Francis Willis.[1] An analysis of the King's hair was carried out in 2005, which revealed slightly raised lead levels and "unexpectedly high concentration of arsenic" (Cox et al. 2005: 333).[2] Cox's article suggests that arsenic levels were in line with the type of treatment prescribed by Willis, but arsenic was also widely used for skin treatments and cosmetics during the eighteenth century (Martin 2009).[3] In 1811, upon passage of the Regency Act, the Prince of Wales became Regent and his father was placed in seclusion at Windsor Castle (Hibbert 1998).[4]

As his physical condition deteriorated towards the end of his life, George III's clothing was adapted to make dressing and undressing easier for the monarch and his servants. One of his waistcoats dated 1819 in the collection of the Historic Royal Palaces in England shows adaptations in the sleeves, where pieces of fabric were inserted to aid mobility. The shape of the top of the sleeves where it joins the body of the garment changes to resemble a type of puff sleeve, which would not have conformed to contemporary male fashion, but it is unclear whether George III would have been seen out in public at the time he would have been wearing this garment. In fact, for a few weeks before his death in January 1820 he was unable to walk or dress himself. The insertion at the top of the sleeve appears to be cut on the bias, and is gathered along the top, where it is stitched into the armscye of the coat, and bottom, where it attaches to the sleeve, the combination of fabric cut and gathering allowing flexibility and space for movement.[5] It is interesting to speculate how this adaptation might be approached today, given advances in fabric engineering and manipulation which might assist in ease of movement, donning and doffing.

King George III's condition was for the most part, concealed from the public, but at roughly the same time period, one of the most famous fashionable figures in England was living a very public life with multiple disabilities. Vice-Admiral Horatio Nelson was Britain's most celebrated naval hero and regarded as one of the greatest naval commanders in history. Nelson's illustrious career included victories at sea against the French and Spanish, and he is celebrated through multiple monuments across the United Kingdom, including Nelson's Column in Trafalgar Square, London. During his many naval campaigns, Nelson sustained a series of debilitating injuries. He underwent a partial right arm amputation as a result of injuries sustained during an amphibious assault on Santa Cruz, Tenerife in 1797; almost lost his eyesight in Corsica; sustained a head injury at the Battle of the Nile in 1798; and was eventually killed in action at the Battle of Trafalgar in 1805. Throughout his naval career, his uniform and other items of clothing were adapted in response to this series of injuries that were sustained during his time on active duty.

Evidence that the right sleeve of his coat was adapted after the amputation of his right arm in July 1797 is shown in several portraits. The appearance of between two and three black ribbons tied in bows on the upper exterior right sleeve is apparent in portraits painted directly after the surgery. Some suggest that the sleeve had an aperture to enable treatment to be given without the painful process of doffing the coat, since there were problems with the healing process (surgeons had been unable to remove one of the ligatures and drainage from the wound needed constant cleaning) and Nelson was in some pain for several months until it came out on its own and the wound finally healed. Others suggest that the opening was added to allow more room and ease of movement for the donning and doffing process. A portrait of Nelson from 1801 clearly shows the ribbons tied around the upper right arm (Fig. 3.1). These ribbons do not appear in later portraits, suggesting that the wound had healed enough so that constant attention from the outside was not required,

Figure 3.1 *British military hero, Vice-Admiral Horatio Nelson, 1801. Image shows Nelson with his right sleeve cuff attached to front of jacket, and upper outside part of right sleeve with bows, indicating that the sleeve could be opened from the outside for his wounds to be dressed. Original Artwork: Engraving after portrait by Lemuel Abbott. Photo by Rischgitz/Getty Images*

and Nelson's jacket sleeve no longer required adaptation for access to the wounded arm. He did continue to wear the full sleeve after the amputation, secured to the front of his coat by a button and loop, anticipating a similar trend used by veterans of the American Civil War by about sixty years.

Interestingly, Nelson is portrayed in an adapted shirt on board ship at the Battle of the Nile after receiving a wound to the forehead (Fig. 3.2). It was

Figure 3.2 *Vice-Admiral Sir Horatio Nelson, attributed to Guy Head, oil on canvas, c. 1800. This portrait shows Nelson injured and bloodied after being wounded in the Battle of the Nile in 1798. Portrait shows adapted shirt to fit amputated right arm of wearer. Photo IanDagnall Computing/Alamy Stock Photo*

unusual for the naval hero to be shown without formal uniform in such a vulnerable situation. Walker describes the portrait as "an imaginary reconstruction" but: "as near as we shall approach to his battered countenance." (Walker 1998: 58).[6] He did not lose his eye, however, he was wounded just above his eye during the battle, hence the bandage over his forehead. Note that the shirt sleeve, which would have been concealed under the jacket, has been adapted for his partially amputated right arm.

There is evidence that his undershirts (again, concealed garments), were also adapted by removing the sleeve completely at the location of amputation on his right arm. The National Maritime Museum in Greenwich, London, has an undershirt showing how the right sleeve is cut about the same length as a modern T-shirt and the edges finished with blanket stitch. The shirt is dated *c.* 1800 and made from wool, linen and silk, according to museum records.

Nelson famously wore a bicorne hat, which was adapted to have a green eyeshade which folded down to shield his good eye from the sun (Coleman 2002: 361).[7] Frustrated by not being able to see while on board ship in bright sunshine, Nelson had written to his mistress, Lady Emma Hamilton, asking her to make him one or two shades according to his design, but it appears that Lock the Hatters of London were eventually responsible for the final product.

The bicorne hat itself complete with shade is in the collections of Westminster Abbey in London (Fig. 3.3) while the original sketch for the shade, following Nelson's ideas, is in the possession of Lock the Hatters (Fig. 3.4).

Nelson lived a fashionable life. He carried on an infamous and public romantic affair with fashionable society beauty Emma, Lady Hamilton, which resulted in a daughter, Horatia. He was given multiple aristocratic titles and ascended into the upper echelons of British fashionable society. He attended the English royal court, balls and banquets of London, increasingly with Lady Hamilton, and their affair became high gossip for fashionable London society and beyond. His death on board his ship, HMS *Victory*, in 1805 despite winning the Battle of Trafalgar against the Franco–Spanish navy, was a huge loss for the English Navy and for the country itself. King George III is alleged to have said upon hearing the news: "We have lost more than we have gained." Nelson's disabilities, sustained through the incessant traumas of an active duty military career, cannot be overlooked in writing this story due to his stature in fashionable society in early nineteenth century England. His wardrobe, which, assigned to a man of distinction and in service to the British Navy, needed always to appear exemplary, most likely would have contained other examples of adaptations to facilitate his public appearances. It also seems as though Nelson himself was responsible for some of these designs.

Figure 3.3 *Nelson's bicorne hat showing sunshade attached to the front designed to protect his eyes in bright sunlight. Courtesy Dean and Chapter of Westminster*

Figure 3.4 *Inside cover of ledger owned by Lock's showing original rough sketch for what appears to be Nelson's visor addition to his bicorne hat. Admiral Lord Nelson visits Lock & Co. for the first time to order a "cocked hat and cockade 7 1/8th full"— his signature bicorne complete with eyeshade. Courtesy Lock & Co. Hatters, St James's Street, London*

The example of Vice-Admiral Nelson and his "adapted" clothing and accessories raise some thoughts for consideration. Could his collaboration with Lock the Hatters be viewed as an early example of co-design? Today's design community is well trained in the practice of engaging the user in conversations from the start of design projects, as well as looking to user communities for input and suggestions, but how common would it have been for a customer of Lock's to have given such direct prescription for a design idea? Would this have been a commonplace aspect of bespoke men's tailoring at the time? Another thought to consider is the attitude towards disability sustained as a result of trauma rather than a lifelong chronic or progressive disease. Later in this chapter I will discuss the pride of US Civil War Veterans wearing their shirt sleeves pinned to their jacket fronts like Nelson, to show that they had sacrificed for the military and their country. This external show of disability through clothing is less evident in the case of people whose disability was not as "socially acceptable" or even "heroic," which would certainly explain some of William Hay's attitude from the previous chapter.

Another British military figure, the 1st Baron Raglan (see Fig. 3.5), whose right arm was amputated between the shoulder and the elbow after he was hit with a musket-ball at the Battle of Waterloo in 1815, was partially responsible for a sleeve design which is ubiquitous in contemporary sportswear. Due to this injury on the battlefield early in his military career, Raglan commissioned a coat from the London-based outdoor wear company Aquascutum to be specially developed with a particular cut and seaming of the sleeve so that he could effectively use his sword with his left arm. The sleeve, nicknamed the raglan, afforded him greater movement and articulation of his good arm because of the extension of the sleeve piece through the body of the jacket up to the collar. Aquascutum, founded by tailor John Emery in 1851 and now a luxury outerwear brand, also outfitted soldiers during the Crimean War of the 1850s (Lord Raglan was Commander of the British Troops during that war), using a new innovative waterproof fabric.

Lord Raglan passed away not long after a failed attempt to besiege the city of Sebastopol in 1855, but the adaptation, which became the raglan sleeve, lives on in today's sportswear, due its superior mobility in the upper body to allow for arm articulation (see Fig. 3.6).

The fact that established clothing and accessories companies, Lock and Aquascutum, had been responsible for creating the adaptations for the Lords Nelson and Raglan respectively is not unusual. Innovation and creativity was not new to the tailoring trade and in fact tailors were taught at an early age how to customize their work. Guidelines for tailors, especially helpful for apprentices, had been published within the trade for many years. In the nineteenth century we find evidence that these publications included instructions for adaptations

Figure 3.5 *Lord Raglan (c. 1840), who commanded the British forces during the Crimean War. Image shows Raglan standing in uniform with his right arm tucked into front of double-breasted coat. Photo by Popperfoto via Getty Images/Getty Images*

to accommodate body sizes and shapes that were not considered "standard." George Walker's 1840 (fourth edition) *The Tailor's Masterpiece* includes sections about pattern adaptations for "Disproportionate Figures," "Irregularly Shaped Figures," and "Hump-backed Persons."[8] *A Practical Guide for the Tailor's Cutting-Room*, published in 1848 by Joseph Couts, included a section on how to tailor for "Disproportioned Persons," explaining:

Figure 3.6 *Modern football shirt with raglan sleeves. Stock Photo, Getty Images UK*

There are few things pertaining to his trade, more perplexing to the tailor, or requiring a greater exercise of skill, than to fit disproportionate figures, so all the parts are not, in such cases, duplicates of each other and yet they must be made, as far as possible, to appear so; it being a part, and important once, of the tailor's business, to conceal the defects of nature … disproportionate figures … will be fitted with the same ease and by the same plan whether very erect and full chested or round backed and stooping or otherwise, the same plan is adopted to measure all and will produce the Garment accordingly in all its bearings corresponding with the figure.

COUTS 1848: 137[9]

Included in Couts' book were directions on "Measuring and cutting for a low shouldered man," "Measuring and cutting for a person with the haunch bone dislocated" (this translates to having a "short leg"), "Measuring and cutting for a hunchback," "Measuring and cutting for a round shouldered man," and "Measuring and cutting for bellied men." The book includes images of pattern alterations that could be used in the tailoring process (Fig. 3.7).

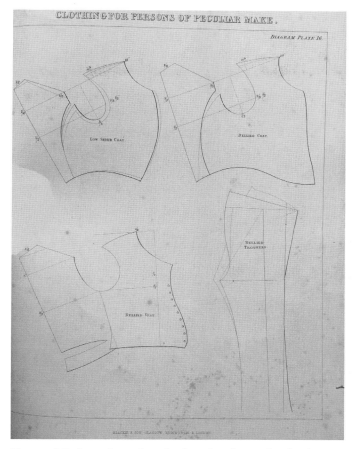

Figure 3.7 *Page from Joseph Couts' tailoring book, showing pattern alteration alternatives for the male body. Photo Credit: Author, 2021*

For women's fashion, the nineteenth century was a time of extensive changes in shape, detail, decoration and materials. Women's socio-economic and cultural status also fluctuated in a Western/industrialized society impacted increasingly by the effects of the Industrial Revolution and the rise of the capitalist economic/political system. Many women experienced subjugation at the hand of societal and legal norms but many were also actively involved in progressive social movements, exhibiting acts of bravery and selflessness to challenge the social status quo. Fashion, however, especially in the first half of the century, was designed to constrict, subjugate, and decorate. Carolyn Day, in her book *Consumptive Chic* (2017) explains how the prominent fashionable aesthetic for women of wealthier families was actually to emulate a weak body, prone to fainting and unable to withstand much activity.[10] Day designated this "Consumptive Chic" based on the effects of tuberculosis (TB), a highly contagious disease that was in reality the leading cause of death in the United States during the nineteenth century. Consumption (the term that was used for tuberculosis), and its symptoms set a "romanticized" cultural style for the female standard of perfection for many years, and offered a bizarre example of how the outward presentation of a disease and its debilitating effects created a fashionable ideal for a generation. More recently, the term "Heroin Chic" was used in the early 1990s to describe the prevailing fashion look of models, whose appearance in fashion marketing resembled the debilitating physical effects of using hard street drugs.

Reflection on the restrictive female fashions of the nineteenth century invites the idea that fashion may have been partially responsible for a range of disabling conditions. Fashionable clothing ranged from fabrics so light at the beginning of the century that they failed to keep the body protected from colder climates, to layers of materials so heavy by mid-century that the weight of fashionable garments imposed undue burdens on women's bodies and prevented healthy exercise and activity. Together with the restrictions of the corset, which was worn uninterrupted through the century with changes in shape and length only, these fashion standards impacted women's bodies with long-term health effects and chronic conditions. The forcing of women's bodies into a shape that is so far from the natural shape of the body, and restricting movement and freedom, again brings to mind the use of waif-like supermodels in the 1990s and the "Photoshopping" of marketing images by some major fashion brands. The imposition of a fashionable ideal on body image, forced on impressionable, mostly young women, has been present for longer than we think.

Along with the evidence that fashion served to subjugate women by disabling their freedom of movement through clothing and accessories, there are instances in the nineteenth century where fashion may have actually transformed the physical nature of women's bodies, beginning in childhood. The Metropolitan Museum's Costume Institute collection includes multiple dresses that account for a lowered shoulder on one side of the body, possibly indicating curvature of the spine. Since clothing was made specifically for the individual prior to mass production in the latter part of the century, these examples may indicate the commonality of body asymmetry, at least among people of fashion. Other museums have indications of children's bodices with shoulders so low that it is suspected that young girls must have developed extremely bad posture and spinal curvature from trying to keep their dresses up on their shoulders. In 1854 Mary Philadelphia Merrifield wrote one of the earliest histories of fashion, *Dress as a Fine art* in which she states: "What pains we take to distort and disfigure the beautiful form that nature has bestowed upon the human race!" (Merrifield 1854: 82).[11] She suggested that low-cut necklines on dresses, which fall off the shoulder, caused women to have spent their lives with one shoulder raised higher than the other, and "the spine is drawn towards the same side. It is said that there is scarcely one English woman in fifty who has not one shoulder higher or thicker than the other." (Merrifield, 1854: 137)

The enterprising London-based inventor and business owner, (Madame) Roxey Ann Caplin, made and sold "Hygienic Corsets" which were advertised as "improving the figure and affording ease and comfort in every period and condition of life." (Caplin 1864: 93)[12] Caplin produced and sold corsets, and patented a variety of other products such as braces, which she promoted as giving support to the back, and keeping the shoulders in the correct anatomical position. In her book, *Health and Beauty*, Caplin offered her opinion on a variety spinal curvatures and proposed solutions based on her product lines: "Let us suppose a lateral curvature of the spine, and that the lady is unable to rise from this position; it will be evident to anyone, that what we want to find here is a point of support, from which the body may be elevated towards the erect attitude: and this we shall discover in the hip or pelvis, from which the deviation has taken place."[13] It is acknowledged that these opinions were tempered with the objective of selling products, but it does offer a picture of the types of posture differences experienced by women at this time. Whether these anatomical differences were caused by fashion, lifestyle or another factor remains unknown.

As the nineteenth century progressed, and fashionable dress was taking its toll on women's body shape and posture, the Dress Reform movement was gaining momentum among activists for women's rights, bringing public attention to evidence that items of fashionable clothing could be harmful to women. These items were believed to cause chronic physical problems that might sometimes result in death. With its formal beginning as a movement in the mid-nineteenth century and continuing until the First World War, the Dress Reformers encouraged fashionable women to change their silhouette and style by adopting looser fitting, lighter weight and less constrictive clothing. The Dress Reform movement paralleled women's suffrage in its intentions and its activism, and can be seen as similar to the activism witnessed in the disability rights movement of the 1960s, suggesting that freedom in clothing and independence in dressing can be effective gateways to progressive developments in many other aspects of life.

In his book, *The Influence of Clothing on Health* (1886), intended as a dress reform manifesto, Frederick Treves recognized and focused on the need for reform to alleviate the fashion practice of tight lacing of corsets and the societal propensity for shaping the female body from a young age: "That it is possible to have a dress that is both healthy and attractive has been proved over and over again." (Treves 1886: 12)[14] Treves discussed how the ubiquitous wearing of the corset may have actually caused disability in the past. He cited concerns around the displacement of viscera (internal organs); restrictions to respiration and circulation; effect on the muscular structure of the torso; and finally changes to the overall shape of the body. Treves also had strong opinions on how fashionable shoes impacted the shape of bones in the foot, and how high heels (defined by Treves as more than three-quarters of an inch tall) shifted the natural posture of the body, so that "the mechanism of the foot is impaired, and undue muscular exertion is demanded in the act of walking."[15]

Despite dress reform activists campaigning to loosen the stays of the Western world, the popularity of the corset as an aid, or assistive device, to correct the "deformed" body was so widespread in the nineteenth century that entrepreneurial companies sprung up to supply fashionable consumers with product options. The Natural Body Brace Co., based in Salina, Kansas, explained its product in a brochure as "an abdominal supporter and shoulder brace to uplift women's bodies ... it takes hold of the whole trunk so as to secure erect posture, maintain proper obliquity of the pelvis, balance the whole body upon its normal axis, and give to every internal organ the support of its natural surroundings."[16] The company encouraged a wide array of people to wear the brace: "All persons, male or female (whether diseased or not), who, on account of weight or weakness, need support or additional strength." The brochure included testimonials from "invalids" who attested that they could now stand and walk due to wearing the brace. Catalogs from companies such as this abounded throughout the second half of the century as people coveted the effects of a device to give them an erect and fashionable appearance. So here lies the corset conundrum, first mentioned in ch. 2 of this book—with dual roles as both disabler of bodies and as assistive device, how should this item of clothing be evaluated in the history of fashion/disability intersectionality?

Charitable Organizations

Nineteenth-century industrialization in Western society affected disability in many ways. Disabled people who had been able to engage in some type of self-actualizing occupation in a domestic setting were not able to transition easily from home to factory when jobs moved to urban environments, thereby forcing many disabled people into a state of poverty and further isolation from society. In addition, industrial accidents (ironically many in the textile industry) were frequently responsible for impairments and long-term disability for which contemporary society was completely unprepared. As an example, in 1898 in Great Britain, there were 3,728 non-fatal reported accidents in textile factories alone and twenty-six fatalities in the same year.[17] To cope with increasing numbers of injured workers, institutions were set up as a way to give disabled people some agency in their lives, and teach new skills so they could be considered "useful." (Nielsen 2013: 74)[18]

The direct impact of this growing institutionalization on fashion may have been minimal, knowing that the working classes, who typically could not have afforded to participate in fashionable life, would have taken the brunt of industrial accidents, not the wealthy and privileged in society. However, there are some examples of the fledgling fashion industry intersecting with charitable institutions that had been established to benefit disabled people. In the second half of the nineteenth century, the manufacture of artificial flowers was booming in fashionable cities such as Paris, London and New York. The workers who made these flowers, most of which were destined for couture fashion houses, hat makers and other accessory trades, were for the most part young girls. "By 1865, there were some 10,000 artificial flower makers working in Paris, 80–85 per cent of whom were women and girls; they accounted for about 10 per cent of Paris's female workforce." (De la Haye, 2020: 103).[19] Flower making involved skilled work which often involved an apprenticeship, and young women who excelled at the practice could continue their career into old age, despite the physically hard work which often involved the use of multiple toxic substances. Artificial flower making was the subject of a charitable training scheme initiated by John Alfred Groom in East London. In 1866, disturbed by the amount of flower sellers who were blind or amputees as a result of factory accidents, he founded the "Watercress and Flower Girls' Christian Mission." Initially the goal was to provide food and washing facilities, however in 1876, he opened a school which provided training for young women to study fresh flowers and make artificial ones. The factory expanded into other parts of the country and continued making flowers until the early 1930s.

3.2 The Late Nineteenth Century: Effects of War

In the second half of the nineteenth century, the story in the United States began with Civil War. The effects of the war superseded class and socio-economic distinction, since the increase in the number of disabled servicemen returning to civilian life crossed all ranks and social classes. Institutions for wounded veterans were established, and the post-war years were witness to an increase in the invention, development and adoption of assistive devices provided to disabled veterans. This increase continued through the latter part of the century. In 1863 President Lincoln and the War Department established the Invalid Corps, whose members were provided with assistive devices including prosthetics, canes, and eyeglasses, and many of these devices found their way into fashionable life.

The largest long-term impact on the veteran population and the biggest survivable treatment was amputation. Approximately 60,000 amputations were performed during the war between 1861–65. Forty-five thousand of these amputees survived to live the remainder of their lives without hands and/or fingers, and full or partial arms and/or legs. Because of the need for replacement limbs for these veterans, the prosthetic industry experienced a steep upwards curve in production and sales. For example, between 1846 and the start of the Civil War in 1860, thirty-four total US patents had been issued for "artificial limbs," "crutches" and "invalid chairs" (precursor to the wheelchair). Between 1861–73, 133 similar patents were issued (Figg and Farrell-Beck 1993).[20] The goal of these artificial limbs was to allow an individual to carry out normal daily activities and to conceal the fact that the individual had been through an amputation procedure. The US Government paid for all veterans' prosthetic limbs after the Civil War.

This same period also witnessed an increase in the popularity of portrait photography, and photographic evidence shows that in spite of the prevalence and availability of prosthetics, veterans did not shy away from documenting their disability through the camera lens. Figg and Farrell-Beck (1993) analysed photos from 1861–1932, examining disabled veterans' adaptations to their clothing, and found that for the most part, veterans did not modify their clothing to accommodate an amputation in front of the camera. They typically fastened their clothing creatively, such as in the case of many arm amputees, who fastened sleeves up on the front of their uniform at chest level, the shoulder or under the arm according to military tradition witnessed with Vice-Admiral Nelson at the start of the century. The photographs gave little indication in identifying the techniques through which sleeves were fastened other than a loop of fabric over a button on a cuff. Fig. 3.8 shows three young men from New England, all Civil War veterans, posing for a photographic portrait in fashionable clothing (frock coats) of the period.[21]

By examining motivations for displaying the loss of the upper limb in this way, Figg and Farrell-Beck explained several possible reasons. The positioning

Figure 3.8 *From right to left: Thomas Plunkett, 21st Massachusetts, a prewar mechanic, a double amputee; William A. McNulty, 10th New York, an arm amputee; and William R. Mudge, 2nd Massachusetts, former photographer, blinded in the war. Photo by Heritage Art/Heritage Images via Getty Images*

of the arm to the front follows the natural bend of the limb, for example, and a forward bent arm mirrors conventional portrait style at the time, with one hand inside the coat (Vice-Admiral Nelson and Lord Raglan were portrayed the same way in photographic portraits). There was little evidence that arm prosthetics were used for photographs, since few are visible in photographs, and since artificial legs were worn with shoes, those also cannot be distinguished from the photographic evidence. The researchers noted from historical sources that soldiers who fastened their clothing and avoided wearing artificial limbs made their disability more noticeable, but in turn were well treated by the public who "no longer treated the veterans as significantly different from the rest of society." (Figg and Farrell-Beck 1993: 468) In fact, in many cases it was socially advantageous to show they had "given a limb" during the war, as these veterans returned home as heroes in both North and South. Wearing fashionable clothing that did not conceal an amputation thus enabled social standing through the visual cue of having "sacrificed for their side" during the war.[22] As a result of the Civil War and the increasing mechanization of Industrial Capitalism, the United States became the biggest supplier of artificial limbs in the world by the end of the nineteenth century.

As well as a sharp increase in the production and sales of anatomically correct artificial limbs for disabled people after the Civil War in the US, the late nineteenth century saw an increase in experimenting with "rebuilding" aspects of the body which were considered "unsightly" and thus unfashionable, using a variety of methods. This rebuilding was akin to modern plastic surgery, which did not become a medically recognized specialty until the 1930s. One example of these practices consisted of the injection of paraffin into affected body areas. In fashionable circles, people who experienced the destruction of the nasal bridge as a result of syphilis (called saddle nose) were seen as being "greatly handicapped, both in their social and business relations." (Haiken 2002: 174)[23] One way of dealing with the collapse of the nasal bridge was for medical practitioners to inject paraffin into the patient's face in an effort to rebuild the affected part. For some time, paraffin was seen as the ideal substance for cosmetic operations (the Botox of the Victorian era?) and its popularity became widespread in the United States. "It was used to fill out facial wrinkles, in one case to create a testicle, and was rumored to have been injected into breasts." (ibid: 174) However, there were many side effects from the use of this paraffin. It had a tendency to migrate to other parts of the body;

it caused paraffinomas, and removal was difficult, resulting in severe scarring. One of the most famous cases was that of American society beauty Gladys Marie Spencer-Churchill, Duchess of Marlborough (born Gladys Deacon). In her youth Gladys had been considered one of the most fashionable and beautiful women of her day, on both sides of the Atlantic. Her admirers included Marcel Proust, who once said of her: "I never saw a girl with such beauty, such magnificent intelligence, such goodness and charm." (Vickers 2020: 120)[24] At the age of twenty-two, prior to her marriage into English aristocracy (the Duke of Marlborough's first wife was another American, Consuelo Vanderbilt), Gladys, who was uncomfortable with the shape of the bridge of her nose, had paraffin wax injected so that she could have a straight line between her forehead to the tip of her nose, based on her studies of Grecian heads in museums in Rome. Unfortunately, the operation was disastrous. The inserted material later slipped to her chin, causing disfiguring lumps in her face, and she was told she would be permanently disfigured at the bridge of her nose:

> In February 1903, news of Gladys's operation was telegraphed form Biarritz across the globe. She was described as being ill "as the result of the unsuccessful subcutaneous injection of paraffin last fall in an effort to improve the lines of her nose". It was stated that this was a not uncommon operation in France, but in Gladys' case, necrosis of the nose bones had set in.
>
> VICKERS 2020: 87

The end of the nineteenth century marked the first time in the Western/industrialized world when fashion became a possibility for the middle classes, whether it was through purchasing items from newly-built retail stores and mail-order catalogs, or being able to make them at home by following a new paper pattern and using a powered sewing machine. This availability and access to fashionable clothing allowed and enabled social mobility and served to cloud the concept of class distinction by appearance. Stephen Mihm suggests that the nineteenth century transformed the way the civilian population interacted through external appearance:

In the process, the importance of personal appearance underwent a profound transformation. Earlier, preindustrial societies had placed a premium on appearance, especially members of the upper classes, whose continued control of the local social hierarchy depended on the ritual expression of power in the form of dress, speech, and bodily comportment.

MIHM 2002: 287[25]

Mihm goes on to explain that the new socially-conscious middle classes established their social order through the art of self-fashioning rather than the opportunity afforded by birth. This new age of appearances did not tolerate anything less than perfection of physical being, and entrepreneurs on both sides of the Atlantic capitalized on this, especially in the advertising of their products. Advertisements from companies such as A.A. Marks, New York, one of the most prolific manufacturers and distributors of artificial limbs in the US, focused on showing how effectively their products concealed any "condition."[26]

Royalty were not immune to the pressures of physical perfection, nor were Kings William I and George III the only monarchs to have benefited from clever manipulations and adaptations of their royal clothing. Queen Alexandra, at first Princess of Wales and then Queen Consort, wife of Edward VII, ruler of Great Britain after his mother Queen Victoria's passing in 1901, was one of the most stylish women in Britain. She also suffered from a debilitating physical condition brought on by a case of rheumatic fever in 1867. She lost her hearing, and her gait and posture were affected so much that she walked with a pronounced limp for the rest of her life (she passed away in 1925). Examination of her court gowns in various collections around the world show that she also had significant curvature of the spine, perhaps related to the sickness suffered early in her life. Kate Strasdin researched Alexandra's gowns in the collection of the Royal Ontario Museum and explains that upon first examination, it appeared as if decorative motifs across the back bodice were incorrectly aligned (Fig. 3.9).[27] However, further observations of the gowns revealed that "rather than demonstrating some failing on the part of the couturier, the . . . motifs were cleverly placed so that the flowers sat symmetrically

Figure 3.9 *Bodice of a state dress worn by Queen Alexandra, made by Morin-Blossier, France. Silk satin with applied design, inserts of chiffon, sequins, diamanté and beads, c. 1903. Photo shows how the overlapping placement of center back panels were aligned when worn on the body thereby disguising the Queen's body asymmetry Photo Credit: ROM (Royal Ontario Museum), Toronto, Canada. ©ROM*

once they were worn by the Queen, thus disguising her deformity ... She normalized her silhouette through structural changes to her dress and so avoided unwanted speculation about her health and well-being." (Strasdin 2017: 46)

3.3 The Early Twentieth Century: War, Therapy, and Industry

During the early years of the twentieth century, entrepreneurial companies and individuals continued to develop products to meet the needs of people who relied on assistive devices to achieve desired posture and silhouette. Patents for new "specialized" functional clothing products were also issued at a fast rate, including for garments that could be considered examples of early universal design.[28] An entry from the 1914 issue of *Textile World Record* documents an "Improved Undershirt" for which a patent had recently been issued, designed for "children or invalids" (Fig. 3.10).[29] The shirt had no fixed fastenings and was easily adjustable, due to the extensions brought over the shoulder and crossing at front to provide support and also "as a brace to throw the shoulders in correct position." The garment also facilitated the donning and doffing processes, in that the whole garment could be laid out flat "on any desired surface and the infant or invalid upon whom it is desired to be placed may be laid upon this back portion, and the flaps and bands carried around the portions that they are designed to cover without unnecessary rolling or disturbance of the wearer."[30]

The growth of patents and a growing interest in the care and management of people who were considered "invalids" in the language of the early twentieth century were accelerated by two significant events that happened in the second decade of the century—the First World War in Europe and the polio epidemic in

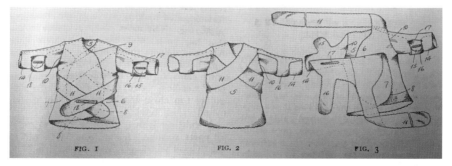

Figure 3.10 *Design for an Improved Undershirt,* Textile World Record, *1914. Image shows patent sketches for a shirt that wraps and unwraps from the body in a system of folds, slots and tabs Photo Credit: Author*

the United States. Both these events resulted in an increase in the number of people needing assistance with clothing, one as a result of injuries sustained on the battlefield or from working with unfamiliar industrial equipment; the second because of permanent effects of the disease on the body, in many cases from childhood. The First World War and its aftermath saw improvement in the quality and growth in numbers of new adaptive technologies; improvements in prosthetics, and increased employment and public attention on disability, in part because there were more people with obvious disabilities on the streets. These two events also gave rise to a change in managed care of disabled people from institutionalization to rehabilitation. Most importantly, rehabilitation professionals and caregivers started to include consideration of the act of dressing and fashioning the body as self-management mechanisms for disabled people.

By the beginning of the twentieth century, many disabled people in the US and Europe were institutionalized. These institutions included asylums (for the mentally ill), colonies, and long-stay hospitals, which had been established to look after patients with emotional, intellectual and physical disabilities. The history of dress in mental health institutions has been fairly well documented, especially regarding dedicated clothing (the straitjacket) as restraint, or "secure dress" (Wynter 2010: 41)[31] In many cases, on admittance to an institution, patients' clothing was removed and replaced with the standardized dress for that institution. Taking away an aspect of a person's identity, including the tools of self-fashioning, has multiple meanings in an institutional setting: standardization and uniformity of patients' appearance, loss of identity, stigmatization, hierarchical management, and treatment through compliance and restriction. In discussing the idea of the total institution, Goffman relates: "On admission to a total institution . . . the individual is likely to be stripped of his usual appearance and of the equipment and services by which he maintains it, thus suffering a personal defacement" (Goffman 1995: 119).[32] Hamlett and Hoskins (2013) explain how in England, institutional patient clothing at the turn of the twentieth century was not significantly different from that of the outside world, but was slower to keep up with current fashions.[33]

The idea of including the act of dressing as an aspect of rehabilitation had been introduced by Granville as early as the 1870s.[34] Granville advocated a move away from institutional uniforms, suggesting that a patient's clothing was a way of reclaiming self-control and authority and that it should become part of a treatment regime, in an early nod towards using clothing and dressing as rehabilitation tools. This idea began to gain real traction in the 1920s. In hospitals for "crippled" children, doctors, therapists, and nurses found that the acts of dressing and undressing improved the physical and cognitive skills of children with disabilities (Hoffman 1979).[35] When rehabilitation gained momentum as a necessary component of integrating a person into society, more sophisticated practices emerged. The incorporation of dressing into an individualized rehabilitative program was found to increase mobilization of joints and muscles. Training was given to caregivers and hospital staff working with children to assist them with donning and doffing of clothing as part of their treatment. It seems that this transition to rehabilitation in the 1920s coincided with a new public awareness and a shift in consciousness towards disability, which represented the beginnings of public advocacy and activism. Other practical opportunities such as working with textiles as occupational therapy became part of institutional practices.

The First World War also spurred a movement for the manufacturing of products by disabled people and the emergence of the disabled maker, selling consumer goods to wealthy customers in a very public forum. Textile-based product design and production had begun to be included in occupational and vocational training for disabled veterans during the War on both sides of the Atlantic, and Nielsen mentions how the US Government established a Committee on Vocational Training for Disabled Soldiers, which gave rise to "rehabilitation industries and vocational programs, 'designed to make cripples successful'" (Nielsen 2013: 129). Chapter 7 will provide a more detailed description of a few of these programs and their modern counterparts, and discuss how makers with disabilities are starting to take their place at the fashion table.

Summary

In this chapter, I have tried to provide some context about this developing hidden history to provoke further thought, discussion and hopefully, further research into the intersection between fashion and disability prior to the twentieth century. Venturing back into historical data is messy and can present conflicting truths, but the main takeaways of what has been discovered and related here can be summarized as follows:

- Fashion and Costume History research has generally omitted examination of how fashionable clothing was adapted for bodies who did not fit social norms

- Existing clothing that was custom made for people of fashion prior to the birth of the ready-to-wear industry gives us clues that there were many more bodies that did not fit in with fashionable cultural norms than has previously been acknowledged

- The lack of identification of pertinent clothing items in collections, together with the stigma that disability brought to wealthy families and the lack of items from the poor, explains some of the difficulties in building a substantive history based on artifacts alone

- The optics of having a fashionable posture and dimensions over time has given rise to many assistive devices such as the corset, which ironically has been both cause and cure of body shape "differences" for centuries. Graham Pullin (2009), in his essay, "Fashion meets Discretion," focuses on the discrete power of the corset.[36] Pullin suggests that the corset has the power to enable without attracting attention, and to empower independence of movement. These two themes of discrete enabling and independent living reoccur in fashion and accessories for disabled people well into the twentieth century

- It is clear that there has been a thriving entrepreneurial industry in corrective devices on both sides of the Atlantic for many centuries. These devices were designed to correct almost any part of the body that did not "conform" to fashionable posture. Current product offerings which have the same goals incorporate new scientific and technological developments in functional and smart materials

- In some ways, the fashion story prior to the 1920s appears more accepting of disability than in recent years. We see this with the broad popularity of Lavinia Warren, a little person who became a mid-nineteenth century fashion icon with cultural appeal, dressed by

noted couturiers Charles Worth and Mme. Demorest, and a wealthy
woman in her own right (see Profile at the end of this chapter)

- The creativity in adapting fashion and creating devices to assist people
with disabilities is evident well before Western industrialization took
control of the industry. William III's hastily-adapted waistcoat
essentially operates on the same principle used today in adaptive
clothing, that is, opening up seams for easy access, and George III's
waistcoat inserts fabric to aid mobility in dressing and undressing, as
well as basic movements. The differences between historic adaptations
and contemporary innovation reside mainly in materials development.
Lacking hook and loop tape (Velcro®), William's tailors relied on ties
and bows that aided in aesthetic appeal, while George's waistcoat
additions were made possible by gathered twill fabric, but could
perhaps have been substituted with a stretch fabric if designed today

- The history of fashion and disabled people prior to 1920 has not been the
subject of much formal investigation, so most conclusions should be
drawn guardedly, including the ones presented in this chapter. In the
research process, I have relied on the knowledge of archival and museum
personnel; forensic-type investigations of adapted historic pieces, and
print, photographic and written source materials. Primary and secondary
evidence suggest that the overall focus was on fashionable concealment
so that bodies could "fit in." It appears that with a focus on concealment,
any type of disability was disguised and/or swept out of sight of polite
society. Further study of garments which have been adapted for body
asymmetry may yield that much more "correction" was carried out on
fashionable clothing than has been acknowledged, and is prevalent in
many collections of historic dress. The art of customization and tailoring
to fit the fashionable body offers an interesting perspective: If the
population was used to adapting clothing to fit bodies, what have we lost
with the birth of the ready-to-wear and the "few-standard-sizes-fits-all"
model? Has the post-1850s ready-to-wear industry actually contributed
to the disablement of Western/industrialized society by removing
people's ability to purchase garments that are specifically designed and
built for their bodies and physical abilities?

Profile: Lavinia Warren

In the nineteenth-century US, traveling shows, which exhibited human bodies as "freaks" to a curious paying public, grew in popularity. The world was rapidly opening up to new experiences through travel and exploration and entrepreneurial types were eager to show bodies which did not conform to the Anglo-Saxon ideal of personhood to a curious and paying public. Lavinia Warren was a proportioned little person turned celebrity; discovered and employed at a young age by P.T. Barnum for his collection of live acts and exhibits of "curiosities" and taken to many glamorous events around the world, for which she had a custom-made wardrobe of contemporary fashions. P.T. Barnum's account of his first business connection with Lavinia Warren in 1862 taken from her autobiography, relates how: "Having arranged the terms of her engagement, I took her to the home of one of my daughters in New York while I was procuring her wardrobe and jewelry and making arrangements for her debut." (Magri 1872: 50)[37] According to her autobiography, Warren was subsequently offered $1,000 per week for her first contract with Barnum, who referred to her as "The Queen of Beauty," and it appears that the label was popularly applied.[38] Fig. 3.11 shows a photograph of Lavinia and Charles Stratton, known to the public as General Tom Thumb, himself an important draw for Barnum's show, on their wedding day in fashionable dress. Images of the marriage ceremony itself first appeared in Frank Leslie's Illustrated magazine, a popular magazine of the time in the US, depicting Lavinia's "Fairy Wedding" ceremony, which took place in 1863 at Grace Church on Broadway in New York City. According to records, over 2,000 guests attended the "lavish" reception that followed the ceremony. It was nicknamed the Fairy Wedding because all four members of the wedding party were little people.

"Madame" Ellen Demorest, head of the Demorest Fashion Empire and a fashion celebrity herself, designed Lavinia's dress. As Ellen Louise Curtis, she had begun her career in upstate New York but soon moved to New York City, where she married William Demorest, a trader who was involved in dry goods and clothing. Together they built Madame Demorest's Emporium of Fashion, and by the time of Lavinia's wedding, the Emporium was regarded as the leader in US fashion design and a supplier of patterns to the trade and home sewers.[39] Knowing how important the Demorest Empire was to the spread of fashion knowledge and practical resources to middle-class America, Lavinia's wedding gown may have made an impact across the country, and the event itself can be considered as an equivalent to today's Instagrammed celebrity weddings.

Lavinia and her husband were admired by a fascinated public. They traveled widely, both in the United States and abroad, and as well as American designers and dressmakers, she patronized Charles Worth's couture house in Paris, which had a dress form (a padded body form used in designing and dressmaking) made especially for her. The City Museum of New York has one dress form of Lavinia's dating to the 1860s and the Barnum Museum in Bridgeport Connecticut (CT) has one that dates to the 1880s. Speculation is that these

Figure 3.11 *The Strattons, G.W.M. Knutt and Minnie Warren (wedding party) with unidentified man. Matthew Brady Studio, c. 1860–70. Photo shows the Stratton and Knutt couples staged and dressed in fashionable wedding party clothes of the 1860s Photo Credit: National Portrait Gallery, Smithsonian Institution; Frederick Hill Meserve Collection*

were used by dressmakers, not Lavinia herself, since she was busy with travel and performance. However, Lavinia had learned dressmaking growing up so that she could make clothes to fit her, and it seems that she had an interest in fashion from a young age. One of her wedding gifts was a sewing machine made for her by Wheeler & Wilson (Bridgeport, CT) that now resides in the Smithsonian Museum (Fig. 3.12).

Figure 3.12 *Mrs. Tom Thumb's Sewing Machine; Wheeler & Wilson.
Photo Credit: Division of Cultural and Community Life, National
Museum of American History, Smithsonian Institution*

Thousands of dollars were spent on her gowns and accessories, to ensure she was dressed in the height of nineteenth-century fashion. Melissa Huber points out: "As her appearance was constantly subjected to scrutiny, dress became an extremely important vehicle through which Lavinia was able to communicate these ideas (a portrayal of education, breeding, success, and culture)." Huber goes on to explain that clothing played a role in "shaping Lavinia's celebrity and positioning her as a tastemaker, albeit one on the fringes of mainstream fashion." (Huber 2012: 22)[40]

In her autobiography, Lavinia rarely mentions her extensive wardrobe, but she does speak of being addressed by a fervently religious woman while on tour with Barnum (date unknown). "Here you are wasting your life in this vain and frivolous manner, puffed up with pride and vanity, adorning your person with finery and gee-gaws" (Magri 1872: 35) and she mentions how, "In those days our dresses were dignified by long trains, which naturally retarded our movements somewhat . . ." (ibid: 177) leaving little doubt that her clothing was on par with the most recent Victorian fashions.[41] Lavinia relates many stories about her fashionable social engagements. On a visit to New York in 1863, she recalls:

> Dinners and receptions galore were tendered us. With the latter I got on very well, for I was accustomed to standing by the hour, but the full-dress, many-course dinners taxed my patience even more than my digestion; and as it was at that time the fashion to eat with gloves on, I found it rather inconvenient, particularly as no

gloves that fitted me could be bought but had to be ordered, and I wondered sometimes whether the sky would fall if the dealer failed to fill my order on time and I should find myself without any that were clean enough to wear.

ibid: 64

P.T. Barnum also outfitted Lavinia's husband, Charles Stratton, known more popularly as General Tom Thumb, in fashionable male dress of the time, although as focus of Barnum's shows, he was more often dressed up in costumes designed especially for him to play the part of fictional and historical characters recognizable to the public. The story of the Strattons and their popularity as a nineteenth-century celebrity couple is fascinating because on the one hand, even in today's supposedly more open and inclusive society, one would be hard pressed to find a celebrity disabled couple with the popularity of Lavinia and Charles. On the other hand, the story should be tempered with the knowledge that at its core, their fame was due to exploitation of their physical appearance at the hands of a skilled showman and entrepreneur, P.T. Barnum.

Notes

1   Peters, T.J. and Wilkinson, D. (2010), "King George III and porphyria: a clinical re-examination of the historical evidence", *History of Psychiatry*, 21 (1): 3–19.

2   17 parts per million, where values greater than 1 part per million indicate arsenic poisoning. For more information, see Cox et al. (2005), "King George III and porphyria: An elemental hypothesis and investigation", *Lancet*, 366: 332–5.

3   Martin, M. (2009), *Selling Beauty: Cosmetics, Commerce and French Society, 1750-1830*, Baltimore, MD: The Johns Hopkins University Press.

4   Hibbert, C. (1998), *George III: A personal history*, New York, NY: Basic Books.

5   Historic Royal Palaces (2023), *Intriguing treasures from the Royal Ceremonial Dress Collection*. Available online: https://www.hrp.org.uk/media/1072/rcdc_top-10_items_2.pdf (accessed January 5, 2023).

6   Walker, R.J.B. (1998), *The Nelson Portraits: An Iconography of Horatio, Viscount Nelson, Vice Admiral of the white*, London: Royal Naval Museum Publications.

7   Coleman, T. (2002), *The Nelson Touch: The Life and Legend of Horatio Nelson*, New York, NY: Oxford University Press.

8   Walker, G. (1840), *The Tailor's Masterpiece; or, The Art of Cutting all kinds of Coats, Waistcoats, Children's Dresses, Military, Hussar, and other Jackets; Gaiters, Gentlemens' and Ladies' Cloaks, &c. &c.*, George Walker.

9   Couts, J. (1848), *A Practical Guide for the Tailor's Cutting-Room; Being a Treatise on Measuring and Cutting Clothing in all Styles; and for every period of life from childhood to old age*, Glasgow: Blackie & Son.

10 Day, C. (2017), *Consumptive Chic: A History of Beauty, Fashion, and Disease*, London: Bloomsbury.

11 Merrifield, M.P. (1854), *Dress as a fine art*, Boston, MA: John P Jewett and Co.

12 Caplin, R.A. (1864), *Health and Beauty, or, Woman and her clothing: considered in relation to the physiological laws of the human body*, London: Kent & Co.

13 Ibid: 145

14 Treves, F. (1886), *The Influence of Clothing on Health*, London: Cassell & Co.

15 Ibid: 104

16 Natural Body Brace Co. (1897), *The Natural Body Brace*, Salina, KS.

17 British Library (1989), Table XVIII. "Reported Accidents in Factories, 1898-Classified according to Industry and Causation". *The British Library Timeline*. Available online at: https://www.bl.uk/learning/timeline/item106751.html (accessed November 15, 2022).

18 Nielsen, K. (2013), *A Disability History of the United States*, Boston: Beacon Press.

19 De la Haye, A. (ed.), (2020), "Permanent Botanicals", in *Ravishing: The Rose in Fashion*, New Haven, CT: Yale University Press.

20 Figg, L. and Farrell-Beck, J. (1993), "Amputation in the Civil War: Physical and Social Dimensions", *Journal of the History of Medicine and Allied Sciences*, 48(4): 454–75.

21 New England Historical Society, (2022), *Cranky Civil War Veterans Return to New England*. Available online: https://newenglandhistoricalsociety.com/cranky-civil-war-veterans-return-new-england/ (accessed December 23, 2022).

22 NIH/US National Library of Medicine (2013), *The Empty Sleeve*. Available online: https://www.nlm.nih.gov/exhibition/lifeandlimb/emptysleeve.html (accessed January 5, 2023).

23 Haiken, E. (2002), "Modern Miracles: The development of cosmetic prosthetics", in *Artificial Parts, Practical Lives: Modern Histories of Prosthetics*, 171–98, K. Ott, D. Serlin and S. Mihm (eds), New York: New York University Press.

24 Vickers, H. (2020), *The Sphinx: The life of Gladys Deacon—Duchess of Marlborough*, London: Hodder and Stoughton, Ltd.

25 Mihm, S. (2002), "'A Limb Which Shall Be Presentable in Polite Society'. Prosthetic Technologies in the Nineteenth Century", in *Artificial Parts, Practical Lives: Modern Histories of Prosthetics*, 282–99, K. Ott, D. Serlin and S. Mihm (eds), New York: New York University Press.

26 A.A. Marks, (1902), *A Treatise on Artificial Limbs with Rubber Hands and Feet*, New York: A.A. Marks

27 For a thorough discussion of this topic, please consult: Strasdin, K. (2017), *Inside the Royal Wardrobe: a dress history of Queen Alexandra*, London: Bloomsbury.

28 See Glossary

29 *Textile World Record*, (October 1914—March 1915), "An Improved Undershirt", 145–6

30 Ibid, p.146

31 Wynter, R. (2010), "'Good in all respects': Appearance and dress at Staffordshire County Lunatic Asylum, 1818–54", *History of Psychiatry*, 22 (1): 40–57.

32 Goffman, E. (1995), "Identity Kits", in J.B. Eicher, M.E. Roach-Higgins and K.K.P. Johnson, (eds), *Dress and Identity*, New York: Fairchild Books.

33 Hamlett, J. and Hoskins, L. (2013), "Comfort in Small Things? Clothing, Control and Agency in County Lunatic Asylums in Nineteenth- and Early Twentieth-Century England", *Journal of Victorian Culture*, 18, (1): 93–114.

34 Granville, J.M. (1877), *The Care and Cure of the Insane*, vol. II, London: Hardwick and Bogue, pp. 174–5.

35 Hoffman, A.M. (1979), *Clothing for the Handicapped, the Aged, and Other People with Special Needs*, Springfield, IL: Thomas Books.

36 Pullin, G. (2009), *Design meets disability*, Cambridge, MA: MIT Press.

37 Magri, M.L. ([1872] 1979), *The Autobiography of Mrs Tom Thumb (Some of My Life Experiences)*, A.H. Saxon (ed.), Hamden, CT: Archon Books.

38 The Barnum Museum, Bridgeport, CT, has a hand-colored illustration published in Frank Leslie's Illustrated Newspaper, on February 21, 1863, showing the marriage ceremony of Charles S. Stratton, known as "General Tom Thumb," to Mercy Lavinia Warren Bump (Lavinia Warren).

39 For a more detailed overview of the importance of the Demorest Emporium, see Walsh, M. (1979), "The Democratization of Fashion: The Emergence of the Women's Dress Pattern Industry", *Journal of American History*, 66 (2): 299–313.

40 Huber, M. (2012), "Barnum's Queen of Beauty", *Costume Society of America Annual Symposium Abstracts*.

41 Magri, L. ([1872] 1979), *The Autobiography of Mrs Tom Thumb (Some of My Life Experiences) by Countess M. Lavinia Magri, formerly Mrs. General Tom Thumb, with the assistance of Sylvester Bleeker*, A.H. Saxon (ed), Hamden, CT: Archon Books.

4

Rehabilitation, Independence, and finally Fashion: 1930s to early 1970s

Introduction

This chapter documents a number of leaps forward taken by designers and researchers during the mid-twentieth century to bring well-fitting and fashionable clothing to disabled consumers. As a result of the combined effects of the polio epidemic in the United States (which began in earnest during the second decade of the twentieth century) and the injuries experienced by military personnel in the First World War in multiple countries, the number of disabled people in the US and Europe rose dramatically by the 1920s. This precipitated an increase in rehabilitation efforts, which included the acts of dressing and undressing. Unfortunately, the economic hardship of the Great Depression in the US during the 1930s affected progress in social programs for the disabled population. Government efforts to alleviate the impact of the Depression and to supply relief to the population through programs such as the Works Progress Administration (WPA) actually excluded people with disabilities because they were categorized as "unemployable" (Nielsen 2013: 132).[1] This exclusionary practice could be seen as akin to similar tactics in eighteenth-century immigration policy in the American Colonies, where disabled people were not considered to be contributing members of society and the labor force and thus barred from entry. However, in contrast to eighteenth-century practices, and because of this and other exclusionary action, citizen activist groups were formed to expose policy inconsistencies and work towards ending discrimination. Clinical and academic research efforts during this mid-century period began to move beyond the exploration of clothing as a self-help tool, to recognition of the importance of the act of fashioning the body and self-expression through design of functional and stylish specialized garments. Research and commercial activities included adaptations to existing ready-to-wear clothing and clothing patterns that could be made in the home. Many of these efforts started as multidisciplinary collaborations and by the 1960s, experts in the fields of fashion design, occupational therapy, ergonomics, and nursing were collaborating on improving skills in dressing and personal appearance. Government assistance, in the form of Agricultural Cooperative Extension Agencies, part of the US Department of Agriculture (USDA) were set up to promote and support research and practice through State Extension programs, many of which were attached to land-grant colleges and universities.[2] Small businesses, some of them run by professionals in the health care and education fields, started to emerge as mail-order suppliers of educational booklets, patterns, and ready-to-wear or customizable fashions for women, men and children. From the late 1960s the voice of the collective disabled population increased in strength and became part of the fight for civil rights to participate in daily life along with all US citizens. This chapter will focus on the evolution from rehabilitation to fashion after the Second World War and the progression of the disabled civil rights movement, focusing on the fashioning of self-identity and the ability to visually self-express as an important aspect of these rights.

4.1 Impact of Work, World War Two, and Rehabilitation: 1925–1950

At the end of the first quarter of the twentieth century, a management approach to disability policy and assistance had begun to emerge which coordinated efforts in awareness, rehabilitation, and program funding at public and private levels. The first large polio epidemic of 1916 in the United States, together with the return and societal integration of disabled veterans from the First World War, had been instrumental in raising awareness of disability in many communities. Simply put, from the 1920s onwards, there were more people with visible disabilities in daily sight of the general public.

Polio, affecting thousands of people, was a disease that began by attacking the central nervous system and then bringing on paralysis. From the 1920s to the 1950s, when a vaccine was developed, polio epidemics continued, affecting thousands in the US, mostly children, and subsequently impacting an entire generation of adults who needed physical and emotional support networks. Many of those impacted became fierce advocates for fully inclusive lives for all people living with disability. The Roosevelt Warm Springs Institute for Rehabilitation in Georgia, founded in 1926 by Franklin Delano Roosevelt as a retreat, was built as an accessible facility, a forerunner to the universal design concept of the built environment.[3]

Clothing was identified as an important tool in the rehabilitation process because it facilitated the mobilization of joints and muscles, and provided practical goals throughout the process (Ruston 1977), thereby acting as a gateway to a participatory life and removing some social barriers.[4] The idea of clothing as a rehabilitation tool gained momentum in the 1920s through the work of care providers who were helping children with polio to lead lives alongside their non-disabled peers. In children's hospitals, doctors, therapists and nurses found that the acts of dressing and undressing improved the physical and cognitive skills of children with disabilities (Hoffman 1979).[5] As rehabilitation was becoming a necessary component of integrating a previously marginalized person into society, more sophisticated efforts were conceived, planned, and executed. Training was given in the 1930s to caregivers and hospital staff working with hospitalized children to assist them with donning and doffing of clothing as part of their hospital treatment. The first signs of conscious recognition that fashioning the self, not just the act of dressing, had a part to play in the full rehabilitation and integration of people living with disability, began to appear, at least in professional clinical circles.

Active fundraising became crucial for increasing general public awareness of disability. In 1919, Ohio businessman Edgar Allen had founded the National Society of Crippled Children, now Easterseals, in order to make a difference in how children with disabilities were regarded in public life. Allen had lost his own son to healthcare inadequacies after a streetcar accident and decided to make a difference in the lives of millions of children and their families. Today Easterseals (the Seals' fundraising campaign for envelopes and letters had begun in 1934) is one of the largest and most recognizable non-profit healthcare organizations in the United States. In 1938, the National Foundation for Infantile Paralysis, now known as the March of Dimes was founded in the US. One measurable outcome of fundraising efforts by the March of Dimes was the increased provision of assistive devices to those who could not afford them, similar to the US government's push to outfit all disabled veterans after the Civil War.

Inventors and entrepreneurs were quick, as always, to provide assistive devices which would engage the user into a more integrated lifestyle. One of these, S.H. Camp & Co., based in Jackson, Michigan, developed the 1934 Camp System of Supports, and offered a reference book to physicians and surgeons, where the development of the system was explained as a "result of the expert knowledge of the handling of textiles combined with continued anatomical study" (Camp System of Supports 1934: 1)[6]. The Camp System produced many types of devices and is an example of one of the small businesses that continued the tradition of providing essential fashion items to the disabled community, some of which continue to this day.

The early 1940s marked a pivotal change in philosophy towards disability in the US, whereby independence and self-reliance were advocated. It was during the Second World War that this change was most evident. The war years saw an increased prevalence of disabled people, not only veterans returning from combat, but civilians, both male and female, who had been injured in industrial accidents. Some of these accidents were a result of people being rushed into the workplace to replace the experienced and skilled labor force, which had been taken to the military front lines. However, the increased need for workers also resulted in an overall increase in the number of disabled people entering the wage-earning workforce. The numbers "rose from 28,000 in 1940 to

300,000 in 1945" (Hahn 1986: 127) and in 1945, a National Employ the Physically Handicapped Week was signed into existence by President Truman.[7] (In the UK, the government had introduced the Disabled Persons (Employment) Act with the same objective—the right to work for disabled people.) Paul Strachan, who was instrumental in the US initiative, further "urged policies and programs that focused on social structures and the ways in which they excluded people with disabilities" (Nielsen 2013: 151), and in 1940 Strachan founded the American Federation of the Physically Handicapped to advocate against prejudice in all walks of life.[8] Public policy began to focus on altering social and employer attitudes rather than increasing rehabilitation and charitable services. With this new access to the workforce, fashion and appearance management were moved into a more prominent place for people with disabilities who now needed modern and culturally appropriate clothes for a variety of workplace settings.

After the Second World War, the changes in philosophy and practice also resulted in an increase in the teaching of independence skills to people with disabilities (Cardwell 1947; Dillingham 1948), and clothing became a key factor for independence training, just as it had been for rehabilitation in the 1930s.[9] Dedicated locations were set up to provide service after medical treatment for the purpose of rehabilitation and training for future employment. This type of training was carried out with patients at the first comprehensive purpose-built rehabilitation center in the nation, the Woodrow Wilson Rehabilitation Center in Virginia, which opened in 1947 (now Wilson Workforce and Rehabilitation Center). President Woodrow Wilson's name was attached to the center for a variety of reasons, but most importantly, he had signed into law the first national rehabilitation program in 1920 (the Smith-Fess Act). Today, the Wilson Workforce and Rehabilitation Center is a cutting-edge facility just west of Charlottesville, Virginia, with national leadership in medical and vocational rehabilitation.[10]

The advances in rehabilitation practice, independent living, and employment opportunities started to bring attention to fashion access for disable people. Before looking at some examples of fashion and disability intersections that started to take shape during the late 1940s and into the 1950s, it is worth taking stock of the state of the overall US fashion industry at this time. The post-war years represented a period of great change for the industry as a whole—American designers were making a mark with comfortable lifestyle fashions, which were completely different from those of their French counterparts (Claire McCardell and Bonnie Cashion are examples of these post-war distinctly American success stories). The industry itself was changing—many European designers had fled to the US during the war, and American involvement during reconstruction in Europe meant that the country was well positioned to take over a portion of fashion leadership and textile production. In addition, the American public was hungry for consumer goods that emulated fashions from Europe but also personified the post-war promise, freedom, and prosperity of being American. American fashion began to move into a lifestyle-oriented phase and to shrug off the lingering, Euro-influenced formalities of the pre-war years.

4.2 Academic and Government-Funded Research: 1950–1973

After the Second World War ended, there were several forces at work pushing to promote the idea that fashion could be accessible to disabled consumers. Initially there was a call for increased proactive intervention by the federal government, such as research funds being steered into Home Economics Extension by the Department of Agriculture (Hallenbeck 1966), resulting in more formal research studies in the field with the intention of information dissemination to citizens of each state in the US.[11] Additionally, activists were starting to demand that attention be given to the problem—no longer was the goal simply for independence in dressing, but disabled consumers wanted to have mainstream fashion within their reach, so that they could visually self-actualize like other retail customers.

Government-funded researchers began to focus not only on the use of existing clothing as a tool to promote independence, but also to address specific clothing problems of targeted groups of people with physical disabilities with a view to developing new products for each group. In 1955, a research project was set up at the University of Connecticut, entitled "Work Simplification in the Area of Child Care for Physically Handicapped Women." The project leader was Eleanor Boettke, who was interested in improving the development of self-help clothing for children and their parents, in order to help mothers with dexterity challenges by promoting dressing independence in children. The project was funded in part by the Federal Office of Vocational Rehabilitation situated within the US Department of Health, Education and Welfare.

Boettke's study involved interactions with one hundred "physically handicapped" mothers and their children. Garments which evolved from the interactions were designed by the research team and then wear-tested by a smaller group of mothers and children. Boettke's work resulted in a booklet entitled "Suggestions for Physically Handicapped Mothers on Clothing for Preschool Children," published in 1957 by the School of Home Economics at the University of Connecticut.[12] The bulletin, which contained "a summary of the design features they found most practical in dealing with the clothing problems of their young children" (Boettke 1957; 2), focused on five areas: Self-help; Growth; Comfort; Wear and Easy-Care. Interestingly, the suggestions in each section were preceded by the phrase "Look for . . ." implying that one did not need to have clothing specially made, but could find it in existing retail stores, with some judicious searching.

Another illustrated booklet resulted from this project, this time focusing on clothing for disabled children, which was entitled "Self-Help Clothing for Handicapped Children," written by Clari Bare, Eleanor Boettke, and Neva Waggoner.[13] It was funded by a grant from Zeta Tau Alpha Fraternity for Women and published in 1962 as a collaboration between the National Easter Seal Society and the School of Home Economics at the University of Connecticut. The booklet was designed to serve "as a guide for parents and professional personnel in the selection and adaptation of clothing for handicapped children," and marked one of the first instances of formal collaboration between academic researchers and trained Occupational Therapists in a project relating to clothing issues. The booklet itself covered a multitude of information, including a preface for parents explaining how to approach "training" a child in self-dressing, independence and the importance of clothing. It explained technical issues such as size choice; fabric types and quality of construction as general chapters, and then focused on specific adaptations to individual children's garments, including underwear, outerwear, footwear, sleepwear, tops/bottoms, dresses, and bathing suits. Every suggestion was accompanied by an illustration. The booklet was reprinted in 1979 as "Self-Help Clothing for Children who have Physical Disabilities," by Eleanor Boettke Hotte, and published by the National Easter Seal Society.[14]

In another important study from the 1950s, Clarice Scott, a Clothing Specialist with the US Department of Agriculture Research Service conducted an in-depth clothing survey with seventy homemakers ranging from twenty-one to eighty-two years in the Washington DC area, all of whom had a variety of physical disabilities. The primary effect of the disability on the body was ambulatory, but for some, hands, arms, and shoulders were also affected. All but seven of the women did their own housework and one-third had children under the age of seventeen in the home. The survey resulted in a compilation of the respondents' clothing likes and dislikes with respect to various styles and design features, which could be found readily available from retailers. Key findings from Scott's survey were the importance of: Comfort, Convenience, Safety, Protection, Serviceability, Fabrics, and Attractiveness. A government-issued bulletin resulted from this research; "Clothes for the Physically Handicapped Homemaker," published by the Agricultural Research Service that contained designs for approximately twenty women's garments, with images and pertinent details about clothing construction for those with the ability and resources to have pieces made up for them or to make them at home.[15] Three dresses (year-round, shirt-waist, hot weather), three blouses (hot weather, raglan sleeve, tailored), three skirts (wraparound, gored, center-front opening), indoor wraps (bolero jacket), slacks, shorts, and pedal pushers (woven and stretch), aprons (low bib, high bib, wheel chair, apron for wet lap work, dress protector for mealtimes) and chair pockets (for home use and for shopping) were described in detail with accompanying photographs. All the products in the booklet were deemed "appropriate" for the 1950s homemaker and her daily activities (e.g., cleaning, doing laundry, and preparing meals).

Commercial dress patterns show similarities with the ideas of these early researchers. According to Hallenbeck (1966), the Simplicity Pattern Company developed a dress pattern (Simplicity 3772, Misses-Women's Sizes 12–40). The

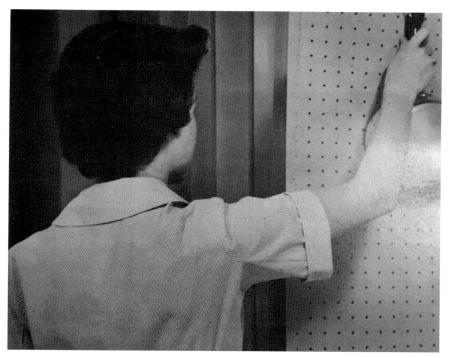

Figure 4.1 *Photograph showing the back view of a semi-kimono sleeve design with extension into the underarm from Clarice Scott's 1961 publication. A model is raising her right arm, showing clearly the seaming in the back of a short-sleeved dress, made from a striped fabric. Photo Credit: US Department of Agriculture, US Government Printing Office (Photographer Unknown)*

dress has an interesting sleeve design, with an action pleat in the front; a lower half that is based on a kimono style, and top half like a set-in sleeve. This would allow for ease of movement in the arms and shoulders, and for donning and doffing. Scott's Shirt Waist Dress, shown in Fig. 4.1, has the same sleeve and its benefit is explained as follows: "Underarm extension of blouse into sleeves provides freedom for reaching without the usual damage to armscye seams." (Scott 1961: 6).

Both Boettke and Scott's work marked the first attempts to target specific groups of women in a "functional" role (homemaking and parenting) and to develop new clothing styles for those specific roles. For the sake of continuity, but a little outside the chronological parameters of this part of the chapter, I will mention a similar study which was carried out in 1969, where forty-six physically limited homemakers with hand/arm and/or leg disabilities living in small town and rural areas of Nebraska and metropolitan areas of New York City were interviewed regarding clothing likes and dislikes (Sindelar 1969).[16] All subjects in the Sindelar study, regardless of their rural or urban status, reported finding it difficult to obtain clothes that enabled them to be independent, explaining that most of the clothing they bought needed to be "remodeled." The rural population actually preferred to sew and adapt their garments in the home. It is interesting to consider the direct line of study from Boettke and Scott and to note that even after ten years between these studies, it appears women's needs were still not being met. The study itself was further published in an academic research journal focused on rehabilitation (Schwab and Sindelar 1973) and marked the beginning of a productive period for this type of inquiry and crossover between clothing studies and rehabilitation studies.[17]

4.3 Independent Designers—Research and Practice: 1950–1960

Despite the apparent demand, many of the first efforts to put clothing into the marketplace were the work of very small entrepreneurial companies whose owners and designers had personal experience with disability. For example, in 1951 Mary E. Brown conducted independent research on the therapeutic value of clothing for teaching self-help skills, and started to work on special clothing designs for children with cerebral palsy to aid in skills development. Her ideas had developed from experiences in her mother's Montessori school in New York City, which she had attended as a child (Hoffman 1979). Throughout the 1950s, the goal of many subsequent initiatives was to assist the disabled population in achieving autonomy through fashionable yet practical clothing.

A pioneering independent organization at this time was the Institute of Physical and Rehabilitation Medicine at the New York University Medical Center, where Helen Cookman was appointed to investigate the clothing problems of patients, at the request of Dr. Howard Rusk, Director of the Institute and considered "the father of rehabilitation medicine."[18] Rusk had opened the Institute at New York University in 1951 and developed groundbreaking practices based on his experiences treating military veterans in the Second World War. His goal was to provide holistic rehabilitation, addressing a disabled person's emotional, psychological, and social needs as well as their physical needs during and after the rehabilitation process. The Institute was the first to deploy a multidisciplinary team approach to the treatment of a patient through the stages of therapy and recovery.

Due to the holistic nature of his approach, Rusk started to become aware and then concerned about the lack of specifically designed clothing for patients with physical limitations and started to make some small-scale experimental studies into the problem. Through feedback and surveys, he found (a) that clothing needed to be easier to don and doff due to lack of patient muscle strength and limited mobility; (b) that clothing needed to be designed for greater acceptance and increased self-esteem, and (c) more durable materials choices for clothing needed to be explored.

Rusk's concern for his patients and their ability to fashion their own appearance in an accessible and culturally acceptable manner led to the hiring of Helen Cookman, an established fashion designer, who was initially tasked with assisting patients whose dressing problems continued past their interactions with the Institute. To carry this out, Cookman coordinated a pilot study, named The Clothing Research Project. Cookman was an established designer of industrial uniforms who was partially deaf, and had made clothing for herself to conceal her bulky hearing aids. Cookman's objectives, however, went further than just helping people achieve independence. She was concerned about producing good quality and fashionable clothing for an underserved group of adults and wanted to see items developed and tested prior to a commercial ready-to-wear distribution program (Fig. 4.2). Cookman is quoted as saying: "It was hard to know where to start, but there was no doubt about our objective—to make a handicapped person look as well dressed as anyone else . . . To me, that meant functional cut with a maximum of eye appeal, classic clothes that would be timeless and economical to manufacture."[19]

A non-profit was established (Clothing Research, Inc. of New York City) to conduct a market survey, design garments and carry out field tests. In 1955 after three years of study, Clothing Research, Inc. presented a specialized line

Figure 4.2 *Helen Cookman presents fashions for seated postures from the Functional Fashions line at the Rusk Institute to the press, 1955. Dr Howard Rusk looks on at right, live models and dress forms are used for display and presentation. The other individuals in the photo have not been identified. Photo Credit: Lilian & Clarence de la Chapelle Medical Archives, NYU Health Sciences Library*

of clothing for men and women with physical disabilities at the American Occupational Therapy Association annual meeting. The line consisted of seventeen "models" for men and women, which had been trial tested over a six-month period at the Institute. The clothes were mostly made from "easy-care" nylon fabrics from Du Pont Laboratories and were constructed with durable stitching techniques. Six items were made available for purchase from a catalog available from Clothing Research, Inc. Apparently the distribution was discontinued at the end of the market testing period, but a new organization, Clothing Research and Development Foundation continued the work and expanded to other rehabilitation organizations in the early 1960s.

Cookman's efforts, while they did not change the focus of the commercial fashion industry in any significant way, did result in a greater awareness of fashions for the disabled consumer due to the press coverage that the project received, and in the development of a self-help book, "Functional Fashions for the Physically Handicapped" (Cookman and Zimmerman 1961), which included detailed descriptions of clothing adaptations and the rationale for each adaptation.[20] The booklet was published by the Institute of Physical Medicine and Rehabilitation. Cookman was listed as "Fashion Designer," while Muriel Zimmerman (a Registered Occupational Therapist) was listed as "Consultant in Self-Help Devices and Homemaking." Howard Rusk wrote the Foreword to the book, in which he speaks of it as the third in a new series of publications issued by the Institute. Helen Cookman's "Message from the Designer" related her observations in her twenty-five year career as a designer and manufacturer "for both the consumer and industrial markets" but she never once mentioned disability in her observations—all her language is inclusive. An example related to comfort reads as follows: "Almost never sacrifice comfort for appearance—to be well dressed you must be comfortable and this means not to be conscious of your clothes" and as related to fabric: "The finest fabric in the world cut off grain will not look well, will not press well and probably will not be comfortable" (Cookman and Zimmerman 1961: 5). Throughout the book, all suggestions are accompanied by sketches with explanations, and sometimes with photographs.

Cookman patented some features developed in the Functional Fashions line, such as a pair of pants with two-way side seam zippers, which was eventually sold at JC Penney in the boys division. Sources of supply were included at the back of the book, as well as basic textile science and care information. The booklet included the results of studies at the Institute, which analysed common dressing problems; general correspondence and inquiries about clothing, and observations and discussions with patients, therapists and nurses. Findings presented in the book showed that 50 percent of patients still had dressing problems upon discharge from the Institute; almost 50 percent of assistive devices were used for manipulating fastenings; and the majority of letters from consumers enquired about Protective Pants, and Shoes. A final summary table provided suggested solutions to individual problems. As previously mentioned, Cookman began to receive press coverage for the Functional Fashions line. By the end of the decade she sensed a need to expand and invited established fashion designers to "include Functional Fashions adaptive features in their own lines" (Wright 2017: 25).[21]

4.4 Connecting Research, Outreach, and Small Business Through Independence and Civil Rights Movements: 1960–1973

The success of the Functional Fashions label led to the founding of the Clothing Research and Development Foundation Inc. (CRDF), a non-profit organization founded in 1960 with Virginia Pope, iconic fashion editor of the mid-century *New York Times*, as President. This was a watershed moment in the history of the intersection of disability and fashion, as it marked the first commercially minded attempt to involve established fashion houses in making fashion accessible and acceptable, backed by a well-respected media presence. CRDF approached several established fashion designers, some of whom signed an agreement with the organization to carry one or more looks in their regular lines that would be designed and labeled as Functional Fashions, for a two-year period beginning in the Fall season of 1963. Fashion shows accompanied these collaborations, and some received press coverage. For example, a newspaper clipping from the October 8, 1963 edition of *Women's Wear Daily* listed the names of some of the designers participating in a "special fashion show given by the Boston Store of Milwaukee and that city's Curative Workshop for the physically handicapped ... Designers include Vera Maxwell, Bonnie Cashin, Davidow, David Goodstein, Tanner of North Carolina, Alexander Shields, and Sarff-Zumpano." According to a piece in *Performance* magazine, the clothes "reflect a tremendous new force emerging from in-depth psychology, the therapeutic power, and deep significance of fashion itself."[22]

The designer Vera Maxwell had the longest collaboration with Functional Fashions, being involved with the project for ten years. As one of the first designers to introduce women's sportswear to the American market, she was a popular designer in the 1940s, 1950s and 1960s. Her obituary in the *New York Times* described her clothing as "casual, comfortable, and classic" (Schiro 1995: B8).[23] Maxwell's famous "Speed Suit," which first emerged on the ready-to-wear market in 1975, was described as being for "the woman who wants to dress quickly" or "anyone whose fingers are crippled with arthritis."[24] There is discussion as to whether the Speed Suit was specifically created for disabled bodies, since it never claimed the Functional Fashions label, but by the mid-1970s the FF label was no longer in existence. It certainly follows guidelines that facilitated the donning and doffing processes, as it was made of stretch knit fabric and was able to be slipped over the head. Schiro described the Speed Suit as "a pull-on dress with a stretch top and no zippers, buttons, snaps or ties." Many versions of the Speed Suit were produced by Maxwell's company throughout the 1970s and a version from 1976 resides in the Costume Institute in the Metropolitan Museum of Art. Vera Maxwell also created the Rugby Suit, which was made of tweed, lined with seal fur, and had a matching lap robe for wheelchair users. The Rugby Suit was designed to fasten with pressure tape (Velcro®).

Bonnie Cashin was another established American fashion designer who collaborated with the Functional Fashions label. Many of Cashin's easy American sportswear pieces were designed for comfort and ease of wear, and her work outside of the Functional Fashions label can be interpreted as accessible and even universally designed. An exhibit at the Milwaukee Art Museum from 2019–20 included her "dog-leash" skirt ensemble (Fig. 4.3). The blogpost for the exhibit explains the skirt as follows: "Cashin designed this skirt, which first appeared in *Harper's Bazaar* in 1957, for a single purpose—to quickly hitch up her skirt with the attached industrial hardware as a way of navigating the stairs at her home while carrying food and drinks in both hands. Functional Fashions later republished it as a sophisticated solution for women with limited mobility."[25]

Cashin also launched a company called The Knittery, which emphasized providing economic aid to disadvantaged groups through the production of highly crafted hand-knits and hand-loomed separates and dresses.[26] "The Knittery was a product of Cashin's passionate belief that anyone marginalized within the workforce, whether by age or misfortune, could learn to knit and contribute something of substance to the fashion world and to their own bank account" (Lake 2016: 212). Cashin also had a working relationship with Lighthouse for the Blind of New York (now Lighthouse International), with whom she developed apron designs to be created by people with visual impairments. According to Lake, some of these aprons are now in museum collections. Unfortunately, the results of her work with these initiatives was not as successful as her mainstream fashion business. With The Knittery, Cashin

Figure 4.3 *Bonnie Cashin, Dog Leash skirt ensemble, 1957. Shown in the Functional Fashions exhibit at the Milwaukee Art Museum, 2019. Courtesy: The Bonnie Cashin Archive, Stephanie Lake Collection*

had hoped to benefit marginalized groups such as older people, disabled people and incarcerated people; however, the workers were confused by a lack of specifications and technical guidance, and there was a long production lag. Lake recounts how Cashin eventually pivoted The Knittery to a luxury service with a long lead time on orders and which became a "labor of love" (Lake 2016: 217). In this capacity, the company successfully served as the launchpad for Cashin's "7 Easy Pieces" capsule collection in 1975, which predated Donna Karan's collection of the same name by about a decade.

Florence Eiseman, another designer associated with Functional Fashions, launched one of the most well-known high-end children's clothing lines in the United States in 1945. Based in Milwaukee, Eiseman's soon became an iconic international brand, and Eiseman products have been worn by the children of President Kennedy, Princess Grace of Monaco, and Beyoncé and Jay-Z. President Obama commissioned the company to design baby gifts that were sent from the White House during his term in office. For decades, the brand has symbolized status, celebrity and affluence. In 1963, Helen Cookman invited the company to collaborate with the Functional Fashions initiative and to create ready-to-wear fashions for disabled children. The collaboration lasted for three years. In her essay entitled "Functional Fashions for Every Child," written for the catalog for an exhibition on Eiseman at the Museum of Wisconsin Art, Natalie Wright explains how the clothing was designed for physical accommodation and "psychological empowerment" (Wright 2017: 25).[27] According to Wright, Eiseman's designs already had features that could be considered "adaptive." For example, Eiseman designs typically omitted constricting waistlines and features such as extra fabric flounces. Eiseman also patented the "add-a-growth" hem that allowed parents to adjust garment length as a child grew. The company created styles with the help of Cookman's research that incorporated universal design principles, such as: wide-leg pants to accommodate leg-braces; reinforced underarm seams to provide stability and prevent wear due to use of crutches; longer dresses to preserve modesty in a wheelchair; side zippers on pants to facilitate bathroom visits; dresses without fasteners that could be donned and doffed over the head, and large shoulder buttons to facilitate fastening. The designs purposefully included features that were "self-help"; which would "teach" a child to dress and undress, and thus instill confidence and self-esteem. The iconic brand visuals such as bright colors and playful appliqués were present in all the designs for the Functional Fashions label. Eiseman maintained that *all* of the designs were functional, and she fought discrimination by including disabled children as models for her clothing lines in company marketing materials. Eiseman ad campaigns regularly showed a non-disabled child next to a disabled child, with both wearing the same outfit. Available for purchase at the same retailers, the differentiation was a Functional Fashions label stitched into each garment. Florence Eiseman continued as principal designer of children's clothing for the CRDF for several years.

Dorothy Cox, another designer involved with Functional Fashions, had been hired as the head designer for Doncaster/Tanner of North Carolina in 1954. Cox had previously designed under the McMullen label for Lord & Taylor, according to a 1949 *New York Times* article.[28] The Doncaster company, which was based in Rutherfordton NC, had started operations in 1931 as the Doncaster Collar and Shirt Co. but soon transitioned to high-end women's clothing and accessories. The Doncaster line was initially sold in conjunction with the Junior League of Charlotte (NC), whose members acted as consultants providing an in-home shopping experience to customers. During the 1950s, Doncaster's in-home wardrobe consultants sold dresses across the country manufactured from high-end Liberty of London fabrics. The Junior League eventually encouraged the company to go into direct sales, and Tanner became the name given to the company's clothing that was sold in retail stores.[29] The company eventually shut down in 2018. Unfortunately, no evidence of Cox's work for the Functional Fashions label can be found at the time of writing, however, the distribution strategy of in-home wardrobe consultation for the Doncaster line aligns with the accessibility in distribution that would have been welcomed by disabled consumers.

Pauline Trigère, another prominent American twentieth-century designer, was also involved in the Functional Fashions project. On October 13, 1962, the *Tribune* (NY) newspaper reported on a fashion show held by the CRDF at a luncheon-conference of the National Multiple Sclerosis Society at the Biltmore Hotel in New York City. Designs shown included Trigère's and Cookman's. One of the models was Mrs. John B. Connors who, according to the newspaper, was named National Polio Mother. Her "bright blue wool dress" was described thus: "It features cape sleeves with high underarm gussets, easy skirt front-zippered to simplify dressing. Deep, roomy pockets eliminate handbag. Shoes are by Capezio." This same photograph was used by the *Cranford Citizen and Chronicle* (NJ) on October 18 to highlight the same fashion show. Mrs. Connors was featured in the media many times during this period.

In 1965 Trigère also designed for the "Help the Handicapped" project, initiated by the Women's Committee of the President's Committee on Employment of the Handicapped to promote and facilitate employment for disabled people. "Helping the handicapped help themselves, they set out to find products these people could make and that the public would want to buy because of their beauty and usefulness. And thus a double-fold result—providing income for these people and public respect for their abilities."[30] The Chair of the Project Earning Power Committee, Mrs. W. Willard Wirtz, invited well-known fashion designers to create designs for articles that the "handicapped" could make. Bill Blass was also involved in the project, and there is evidence that a show was held at the Palmer House in Chicago. Like the Painted Fabrics initiative in the 1920s and 1930s detailed in ch. 7, this project involved established designers creating designs to be made by disabled people and sold to the public. No evidence is available regarding the benefit, monetary or otherwise, to the disabled population involved, or the longevity of this project.

According to various sources, some other designers and brands whose names were associated with the Functional Fashions label included: David Goodstein, of Goodstein Bros and Co.; Sarff-Zumpano, and the William H. Davidow and Sons company, founded in 1880 and known for their tailored coats and suits. Most of these other companies were located in and around New York City, however, at the time of writing, no evidence could be found of existing products with the Functional Fashions label for any of these companies. It is difficult to assess the impact of the Functional Fashions label in contemporary terms due to the differences in the US fashion distribution model in the early 1960s compared with today's system. Helen Cookman's intentions, which were to make fashion accessible to men and women with disabilities, were successful in that she managed to engage and coordinate a group of known designers to design pieces under one label. This in itself is a significant achievement in the fashion world, and the products themselves appear to have hit the mark in terms of aesthetics and functionality. However, we are missing the voice of the customer in this initiative. The reasons for this are unclear. According to Hallenbeck, assessing the program's impact in 1966, the CRDF was presented with multiple challenges in manufacturing and distributing goods associated with the project. Hallenbeck concluded: "No mass market exists for specialized clothing for the physically handicapped . . . there is not such a large market for these specialized items of clothing as was anticipated . . ." (Hallenbeck 1966: 37).[31]

Given today's online retail environment, social media and word-of-mouth (WOM) marketing methods, it is interesting to speculate how Cookman's efforts would have been received if the Functional Fashions label had persisted into the contemporary era.

Design and development did continue under the FF label through the 1960s. Cookman continued to work with existing designers to develop and produce fashion lines for disabled people and she also patented some of her own inventions, a unique activity in the world of fashion products. According to archival information Helen Cookman patented the idea for a pair of jeans in 1960, but spent time searching for partner brands to develop the product so that it could be sold. She eventually found a collaborator in the Levi Strauss company and received funding from the Levi Strauss Foundation.[32] Levi's would go on to offer collaboratively-designed functional jeans in the early 1970s (using Cookman's Trousers for a Handicapped Person) (Fig. 4.4) direct to consumers through special-order brochures at doctor's offices, hospitals and rehab clinics. No sales figures or distribution details are known; however, the pants were priced at $24.50, which in 2022 terms would be about $160.

Despite the lack of follow-through information and breakdown in distribution systems, which prevented Functional Fashions products from getting into the hands of the people who needed them, researchers and historians working in this area are of the opinion that the story of Helen Cookman and her label is of utmost importance and remains the largest collaborative effort in the United States to create fashionable and accessible clothing for disabled people.[33] More space and time would have permitted research into sales figures,

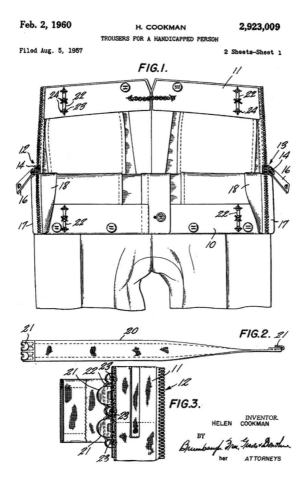

Feb. 2, 1960   H. COOKMAN   2,923,009

TROUSERS FOR A HANDICAPPED PERSON

Filed Aug. 5, 1957   2 Sheets-Sheet 1

Figure 4.4 *Patent for Trousers for a Handicapped Person, by Helen Cookman, 1960. The image shows technical drawings for the inside of pair of men's pants and details of the fastening. Courtesy United States Patent and Trademark Office*

distributors and extant examples, unfortunately the body of work is fragmented. At the time, the movement certainly spread across the country and may have impacted many other efforts. A newspaper article (date unknown) features a TV show about clothing designs for the handicapped modeled by local women in the Des Moines and Ames (IA) area. An Iowa State University extension clothing specialist, Opal Roberson, showed pattern adaptations and a kit of free information was offered on the show. The designers featured in the fashion show all worked through the CRDF for the Functional Fashions label. Two other fashion "houses" are mentioned in the article—the Vocational Guidance and Rehabilitation Service (VGRS) in Cleveland, Ohio, and the Fashion-Able lingerie label in Peoria, Illinois, both of which took up the mantle in championing fashion and accessibility through the latter half of the 1960s.

The VGRS began producing garments in 1962. The initiative began when the head of the sewing department, Dorothy Behrens, at the request of local nursing home administrators, started designing back-opening dresses for elderly patients so that they could have an alternative to hospital gowns. VGRS subsequently carried out collaborative work with Highland View Hospital, a progressive rehabilitation facility in Cleveland, so that garments could be tested for efficacy. Seventeen garments had been designed and produced by 1963 and these were then shown at the National Rehabilitation Association Convention in Miami Beach that year. In January 1964, a "Specially Designed Clothing Service" became a permanent part of the VGRS with Behrens as director and designer. Behrens' work resulted in a mail-order catalog, which included a measuring chart and price list for over forty garments for women, men and children. The items included dresses, skirts, blouses, coats, slacks, and shorts. It should be noted that this represents a change in language from "Handicapped" to "Special" to distinguish the type of clothing in question.

Behrens' designs could be viewed as early examples of "universally" designed garments, as several features were incorporated into a single garment to serve more than one type of physical disability. For example, a dress originally designed for older women with continence concerns was found to be equally suitable for people seated in a wheelchair because of its full cut and overlapping skirt panel. Original sales sheets (see Fig. 4.5) show an available line of six dresses, a tailored skirt and tailored blouse, robe, slip, aprons, men's pants, and shorts with prices ranging up to $30.

Phyllis Hallenbeck, whose work has been cited frequently in this chapter, was a research associate at VGRS. Hallenbeck identified the perceived problem of the intersection of the fashion industry and disability:

Mass production becomes less and less practical as age and sex are considered ... the problem of producing special clothing is made so

VGRS SPECIALLY DESIGNED CLOTHES
What they are and Why we offer this service

Daily, at the Rehabilitation Center of Vocational Guidance and Rehabilitation Services and in the community, we see the tremendous need for clothing which would be easier for dressing and would afford comfort and features in styling to meet various physical needs. Constantly, we are asked to help or assist in meeting special clothing needs in addition to our other services. Because we have a sewing workroom and clients who have been skillfully trained in sewing, it is possible to produce clothing design ideas which were found to be useful and helpful. As a result, we were asked to expand and offer these designs nationally. After consulting with stores and manufacturers, it appeared the most direct and practical way

to offer this service nationally was by mail-order. We are adding new items continuously and this folder shows some of the latest designs. All of the VGRS items are not illustrated but you may request additional information. Because our experience indicates that many of you require made-to-measure garments, please follow the measurement chart carefully. In this way we can assure satisfaction.

We hope that our effort to supply these lovely items in quality fabrics and fine workmanship will provide some solutions to your dressing difficulties. Perhaps a friend or relative could also use these items.

For the walker . . . Convenient carry-all to carry items you use constantly. 5 graduated size pockets for eyeglasses, memo pad, cigarettes; 1 large pocket for magazine, knitting. Fastens to walker with Velcro® Double-stitched, washable denim with coordinated stripe. Green, red, blue, gold, tan, rust. #C-6, $3.95.

For the wheelchair . . . Compact carry-all to keep articles within arm's reach. 4 assorted size pockets for eyeglasses, tissues, coin purse, small radio and books. Velcro® tabs anchor to chair-arm. Carry-all will not interfere with wheelchair operation. Sturdy washable denim. Green, red, blue, gold, rust. #C-5, $3.95.

OTHER VGRS DESIGNS AVAILABLE . . .
Write For Additional Information

#26 Easy-On Blouse	$ 6.95
#212 Flared Skirt	$ 6.95 & $ 8.95
#103 Coachman Dress	$14.95
#132 Men's Shorts	$ 8.95
#160 Duster	$ 8.95
#195 All-Weather Coat-Cape	$21.95
#196 All-Weather Coat, with sleeves	$29.95
Zip-in Lining, both styles #195, #196	$10.00
#A-1 Arm Sling-single, left, right arm	$ 2.95
#A-2 Arm Sling-double, left, right arm	$ 3.95
Bath Lift, assist in transfer	$ 7.95

VOCATIONAL GUIDANCE
and
REHABILITATION SERVICES
REHABILITATION CENTER
2239 E. 55th Street
Cleveland, Ohio 44103

Figure 4.5 *VGRS original line and pricelist, date unknown. The line list includes information about the clothing, a list with style numbers and prices in dollars. Courtesy Vocational Guidance Services, Photographer unknown*

complex by factors of age, sex, ability for self-help, type of physical disability, occupational needs, individual preferences in clothing, and size and body proportion that designers or manufacturers might well be dismayed by the variety of problems involved.

HALLENBECK 1966: 35

As a side note, to follow up on Hallenbeck's opinion from the mid-1960s, I have certainly found in my own work in the first two decades of the twenty-first century that manufacturers, if not "dismayed," are certainly not as familiar with clothing that is factored by age and ability, and this lack of familiarity can lead to a reduction in interest to get involved.

Other organizations and small start-up businesses began to focus on design and production of clothing for specific needs during the 1960s, including Fashion-Able, founded in New York in 1965 by Mrs. Van Davis Odell. This company designed and sold undergarments for ambulatory women with disabilities. The business idea was based on the personal needs of Odell, who had suffered a cerebral aneurysm that left her paralyzed on one side of her body. Subsequently she had difficulty finding suitable underwear products. When she started the business, she could find no marketing research about her target customers, so she concentrated on her own needs, discovering that many others had similar problems. The line of undergarments came in standard contemporary retail sizes and included bras, girdles, slips, robes, and pajamas. The business later expanded into a full line of women's clothing and other items to assist with Activities of Daily Living, with all products available to order through a catalog. The items were first sold through the Helen Gallagher-Foster House mail-order company and in 1971 the business was sold.

The needs of the male disabled consumer were not forgotten during this time of activity of trying to increase fashion product offerings at the retail level. Leinenweber custom tailors, based in Chicago, opened its doors in 1938, and had started tailoring for wheelchair usage in 1944. The owner of the company, William T. Leinenweber, was himself a wheelchair user. The Leinenweber order sheet for suits (which were cut for a seated posture) allowed a customer to select: jacket lapel shape, pocket type, length of jacket, shoulder type, posture, seat type, leg urinal, and height of back pant waist. The catalog read: "Today there is no real reason why a wheelchair man can't have 'that tailored look' like everyone else ... Like all good custom tailored suits, yours has to be adjusted to accommodate your problems in a neat fashion."[34] As well as their measurements, people were encouraged to send in a picture of themselves when they ordered a product. In the mid-1960s, Leinenwebers carried out their own research and worked with rehabilitation centers nationwide.

Another mainstream US-based fashion retailer who became involved in selling clothing and accessories to the disabled consumer was JC Penney. Penney's informational color magazine with many fashion tips, fabric swatches and dressing ideas, entitled "Fashions and Fabrics," included an article in the Fall/Winter 1961 issue entitled "New Function for Clothing—Help for the Handicapped," in which the work of Rusk, Cookman, and Clarice Scott is profiled.[35] In addition, the article summarizes main style features from both projects with photographs, advocates for home sewing help and gives advice for shopping. "Informed, intelligent shopping … could be a great service, and could be done on a volunteer basis, either through individuals, or through … a local rehabilitation center … The question is how can those of us who are well best serve the need."[36]

4.5 Other Activist Efforts and Government Initiatives

In addition to expanded research activity and increased practical options, the 1960s bore witness to an increased number of national seminars and conferences focused on the clothing needs of disabled consumers. The unique aspect of these collective events was their interdisciplinary nature. Home economists, rehabilitation workers, social services workers, as well as professionals from the US Department of Health, Education and Welfare, gathered together as teams with a common goal of "… restoring the handicapped to productive family and community life and to define the need for research and education programs" (Hoffman 1979: 30).[37] On October 9, 1962, Eunice Heywood, Director of the Division of the Division of Home Economics Programs at the Federal Extension Service in Washington DC announced that extension home economists would be cooperating with state and local public assistance agencies to help the physically handicapped with clothing problems, work simplification and nutrition. This meant that Federal Extension Services could provide educational services to families and individuals with disabilities, and throughout the 1960s, extension home economists worked to develop pioneering research programs, with the focus on independent living and self-help through functional clothing.

Many of these Federal Extension Services held conferences and workshops to help deliver information to consumers, caregivers, and educators. Some states also published extension bulletins to provide information to assist people who were disabled. One of these bulletins was *Clothing News and Research Findings* developed by Bernice Tharp at Pennsylvania State University Cooperative Extension, funded by the US Department of Agriculture.[38] In a January 1964 edition titled "The Handicapped—Clothing Implications," Tharp explained how in 1953 she had carried out a survey of national health organizations and agencies which revealed "little documented information on clothing for the physically handicapped," but she found progress being made at the New York State University Medical Center for Rehabilitation in personal care, grooming, and aids for dressing and undressing.[39]

Tharp had completed her Masters Degree at Cornell University in 1956, researching "Design and Fitting Problems in Clothing for the Asymmetric Figure." In the Penn State bulletin, Tharp explained that since many adaptations were beyond the skill level of most home sewers, there was a need for Extension home economists to assemble a set of background information, catalogs, and ready-to-wear pricing information from existing stores that carried "Functional Clothing." The bulletin described what features to look for when considering disabled consumer needs, and suggested procedures for adapting clothing, taking measurements, and maintaining standards for well-fitting clothing. There was also a list of patterns for making the clothing in the home, which could also be used for teaching purposes. The bulletin was designed for Home Economics Extension professionals interested in the subject matter. It is interesting to note that a report on Thalidomide is provided in one edition after Tharp's visit to Canada, where this drug affected many women and children. Thalidomide had not been approved for use in the US, but was responsible for thousands of children being born with birth defects in Europe, Japan, Canada, and Australia in the early-to-mid-1960s.

Many other universities and educational groups published similar bulletins throughout the 1960s, sharing and replicating this government-funded information. The Nebraska Heart Association, together with the Extension Service of the University of Nebraska, published "Easy Fashions for You" (Bulletin EC66-2208) directed towards "Physically Limited Homemakers." The bulletin gave advice on Easy-on/Easy-off Features; Comfort and Freedom of Movement Features; Easy Care and Long Wear Features and Self-Help aids for Homemaking and Daily Activities. The pioneers involved at Nebraska were Audrey Newton (Chair of the Department of Textiles, Clothing and Design) and Extension service agents A.M. Burton and V.Y. Trotter. In Texas, a Texas Tech Textile Research Center brochure, entitled "The Natural Creations," sold garment patterns for between $1.15 and $4.00. The designs, made by Kay Caddell, included a ladies' smock, jumper, dress, wraparound skirt, and blouse, wrap slacks, gown, men's jacket, jeans, and a jumpsuit.

Towards the end of the decade, these multiple efforts across the United States began to pay off in terms of national recognition. On April 27 and 28, 1967, there was an Annual Meeting of The President's Committee on Employment of the Handicapped in Washington DC, which included a panel on Handicapped Homemakers. The three panelists were Dorothy Behrens (VGRS, Cleveland), William T. Leinenweber (Leinenwebers) and Virginia Pope (*New York Times*/CRDF). During the meeting, panelists exhibited fashion products that had been developed by organizations and spoke to the necessity of including clothing and accessories in conversations relating to disability.

As all this was happening, the disability rights movement had also taken shape and was focused on convincing both public and private institutional bodies that social conditions and attitudes caused disability, not the individual medical conditions. Out of this came the Independent Living movement, "organized on the principles of self-determination, consumer control, and deinstitutionalization" (Nielsen 2013: 163).[40] The movement's work to remove barriers resulted in part in the 1968 Architectural Barriers Act, and then the Rehabilitation Act of 1973, which was much more effective and measurable in its results mostly due to its Section 504 language: "not be denied the benefits of, or be subjected to discrimination under any program or activity receiving federal financial assistance" (Nielsen 2013: 166).[41] Section 504 was the first federal legislation designed to remove discrimination against disabled people and improve access to services provided by the United States federal government.

On the other side of the Atlantic, in 1969, Joan Lord of the Shirley Institute, Didsbury, Manchester, was performing pioneering research on clothing for disabled people in the United Kingdom. Nothing of similar scope had been attempted previously in the UK: "Past efforts had little impact due to a lack of communication between investigators and the ultimate user. In the United States, a similar communication problem exists: companies manufacture clothing for the disabled, but there are no compiled lists of these companies or their products" (Johnson, 1972).[42] The outcome of Lord's efforts was a catalog of garments available on the market designed for or suited to handicap and disability. Garments were wear-tested in hospitals or at the Shirley Institute.

> The results of research must be communicated to those who have need of it. Mrs Lord has been of great service by compiling available material into two catalogs which are in turn available for purchase. There is no such "clearing house" to my knowledge in this country. Catalogs are few and difficult to find. Every effort must be made to make tangible the result of research and to not be satisfied with buying them in the annals of journals.[43]

Joan Lord is also responsible for a 1970 monograph on the subject: "Clothing for the handicapped and disabled in hospital or in the community: a review of world literature 1937-1970" published by King Edward's Hospital Fund for London, which is described as follows: "This document reviews the literature written about the use, provision and design of specialized or adapted clothing for people with physical disabilities. Chapters in the report cover the development of special clothing and adaptations; experiences and experiments in hospitals; experience in various countries; fabrics; laundering and dry cleaning; incontinence."[44]

The Disabled Living Foundation, another UK organization, based in London, assembled a Clothing Advisory Panel, which in the late 1960s suggested two projects—one for the "Handicapped Child" and one for the "Handicapped Adult." The resulting publication from the second study, "Clothes Sense—For handicapped adults of all ages,"[45] published in 1973, was comprehensive in scope, covering: Selection of Clothes and Fabrics; Independence Aids; Alterations; Types of Clothing (categorized with illustrations); Storage; and further resources, such as suppliers. As far as I am aware, at the time of writing there has been no update to this publication in the UK.

Summary

This chapter outlines a few of the major milestones that helped move the fashion and disability discourse forward during the mid-twentieth century. The arc of this period, stretching from the polio epidemic and the use of clothing for rehabilitation in the 1930s to the passage of the Rehabilitation Act of 1973, covers much innovation, perseverance and effort by individuals and organizations. The main suggested takeaways for readers are as follows:

- Despite the beginning of the period having some overlap with the previous chapter, it was necessary to set the stage for the reasons behind the rehabilitation work of the 1930s, which used clothing to help with greater independence. It seems as though, for the early pioneers of equal rights for disabled people, clothing was important in a very functional way, but not crucial to the cause. It was not until the Second World War and the increase in opportunities for people with disabilities to go "out to work," that fashion became a consideration, and public awareness grew so that efforts of the 1960s and early 1970s for disabled people to be able to self-fashion were recognized on both sides of the Atlantic

- In addition to this change in awareness and perception, fashion itself became easier to wear after the Second World War as notable fashion designers like Bonnie Cashin and Vera Maxwell epitomized an easy-wear, easy-care style of dressing which was smart but not formal. American consumers, while still fascinated by the ever-changing European dictates of haute couture and licensed designers, were eager to find a style that was unabashedly American, comfortable and affordable. This casual feel was well suited to innovation in universal dressing and adaptation for disability. This tradition is still a hallmark of American fashion, epitomized by many "lifestyle" brands available globally

- The government funding funneled through various agencies to support research and extension made a big difference in the progress of fashion for disabled people during the 1950s and 1960s. Land-grant universities in the United States, with a broad democratic mission to educate all citizens in every state in an accessible manner, were pioneers in this work. There was a wealth of collaboration between academia and private organizations, and these projects gave rise to bulletins, designs, publications, and conferences

- Designers and researchers educated in this system focused their work on people who were not necessarily at the forefront of public or fashion awareness, such as disabled mothers with children and disabled homemakers

- Designers working with the Functional Fashions label showed early evidence of Universal Design principles, such as in Vera Maxwell's dog leash skirt and Florence Eiseman's inclusive childrenswear lines

- Recognition is also due to significant pioneers without whose behind the scenes work the legacy would not be as rich: possibly the first disabled "supermodel" in Mrs. John B. Connors; important advocates from within the fashion industry such as Virginia Pope of the *New York Times*; and rehabilitation professional and visionary Dr. Howard Rusk, who hired Helen Cookman, equally visionary designer, to provide strength for the movement and engage named designers in her work

- Throughout this period, the small entrepreneurial companies that had provided disabled consumers with assistive devices for many years continued to have impact, and were forerunners of the small businesses which started to fulfill the need for accessible fashion for all in the last quarter of the century

- Companies addressing the fashion needs of disabled consumers were designing and selling multiple product categories but primarily through mail order and catalogs and home sales. The Functional Fashions label itself never found a mainstream retail home. Distribution and marketing were spotty, and although the amount of government and academic bulletins, catalogs, conferences, and committees increased through the 1960s along with the civil rights movement, it is not clear that the word was getting out to the people who really needed the products. Undoubtedly, awareness increased for the general public about the prevalence of disability in their communities, but fashion did not seem to be an important part of that awareness. With all the efforts being made to make fashion part of the life of disabled people, it is surprising that by the end of the 1960s there were still no mainstream fashion lines and retailers regularly serving the disabled market as part of their target clientele. The ableism of the fashion industry was still firmly entrenched.

Profile: Frida Kahlo

The artist Frida Kahlo represents a twentieth-century voice from the past who was challenged on a daily basis by multiple disabilities, and yet presented a creative individual persona through her expressive dress, hair, and make-up. Her career as a painter and her marriage to the painter Diego Rivera is well documented and her work continues to draw large audiences at exhibitions worldwide. Her choices of different styles of dressing throughout her life, including the adoption of long skirts and simple geometric blouses worn by indigenous women from the Tehuantepec region of Mexico, as shown in the 1937 photograph of her and Diego (Fig. 4.6), show her creativity in combining aesthetics with functionality into a distinct personal style. It is debated how much of the proactive wearing of these clothes was directly a result of political activism, how much was related to ease of use in donning, doffing and comfort and how much perhaps personal preference and choice in self-expression. This section will unfold some of the aspects of her wardrobe in the context of disability.

Born in 1907, Kahlo contracted polio as a child at age six, which resulted in her right leg being shorter than her left. In 1925 she was severely injured in a bus accident, which left her with multiple physical limitations and a lifetime of surgeries with prolonged periods of bedrest. In a letter to Alejandro Gomez Arias she relates her experiences: "April 31 [1927], Sunday ... they put the plaster cast on me, and since then it's been a real martyrdom that is not comparable to anything else. I feel suffocated, my lungs and my whole back hurt terribly; I can't even touch my leg. I can hardly walk, let alone sleep. Imagine, they hung me by just my head for two and a half hours, and then I stood on my tiptoes for more than one hour while [the cast] was dried with hot air; but when I got home, it was still completely wet." (Kahlo and Zamora 1995: 29).[46]

Although much attention has been paid to the way that Frida dressed and visually self-expressed, little has been written about the intersection of her self-fashioning

Figure 4.6 *Mexican painters Diego Rivera (1886–1957) and Frida Kahlo (1907–54) talk together in the garden, near the porch of Kahlo's home, Mexico City, Mexico, 1937. Frida Kahlo wears a long-sleeve, high-necked blouse and a long skirt in a traditional Tehuantepec style. Photo by FPG/Getty Images*

choices and her disabilities. In 2004, Frida's dressing room at her home, "Casa Azul," was unlocked, fifty years after her death as stipulated by Diego Rivera. Many personal items discovered were cataloged by Rosenzweig, who writes: "In the bath tub was the prosthesis for Frida's right leg, on the end of it a red leather boot adorned with Oriental fabric; from its straps hung tiny bells, now silent, absent the motion of a wearer." (Del Conde 2008: 13).[47] Frida had the boot made for her in 1953 after her leg was partially amputated (Fig. 4.7) The first exhibit that was held to show these newly-discovered pieces ("Appearances can be deceiving: The dresses of Frida Kahlo" at the Museo Frida Kahlo), proposed that "Kahlo's fashion choices were guided primarily by disability, by a need to hide her body's imperfections and gain a sense of comfort and belonging. It presents Kahlo and her suffering body as a sort of 'dark' muse for today's fashion designers." (Aragón 2014: 519)[48] Aragón even suggests that the act of dressing herself may have been therapeutic for the artist.

Kahlo turned to the clothing of indigenous people as a symbol of her Mexican roots, and because the garments were not mass-produced, this gave her self-fashioning

Figure 4.7 *Lace-up boots c.1950 as displayed during the Victoria and Albert Museum's exhibition entitled "Frida Kahlo: Making Her Self Up." The red leather boots are laced up the front and highly decorated on the upper. The right boot has Frida Kahlo's prosthetic leg inside it, above which and attached to it is a leather thigh strap with hinges at the knee. Photo by DANIEL LEAL/AFP via Getty Images*

choices somewhat of an avant-garde, almost haute-couture status. The clothes of her mother's culture (Tehuana), which helped to mask her disability because of their simple, loose design, were also rigidly traditional in shape and motif. Kahlo's use of the two-piece outfits (loose top and a full skirt) favored by Tehuana women, allowed her to roll fabric up and down for medical examinations and to access the supportive structures that she wore underneath.

Teresa del Conde writes: "Frida commented regarding her wardrobe: 'In another era of my life I dressed as a boy, in pants, boots, jacket . . . but when I went to see Diego, I wore a Tehuana outfit. I have never been to Tehuantepec, nor has Diego wanted to take me there. I have no relationship with its people, but among all of Mexican dress, the Tehuana costume is my favorite, and that is why I dress like a Tehuana.'" (Del Conde 2008: 26)[49] Marta Turok in the same catalog explains how the indigenous clothing, possibly suggested by Diego Rivera, suited her situation: ". . . the skirt covered her legs (the weak point of her anatomy, along with her spine) and gave her full mobility despite the corsets she was forced to wear. The style even inspired her to create several outfits and models with the help of her seamstresses . . ." (Turok 2008: 55)[50] Turok (2008) specifies that she also had many other styles of garments hand-made by seamstresses. In a letter to her mother dated March 12, 1931, written while she and Diego were visiting the west coast of the United States, Kahlo states: "I already found a Chinese dressmaker who is going to design two dresses for me, because I don't even have one, the only thing is that they charge a leg and an arm, but there is no other way, because I don't have a sewing machine and I don't know how to design them; she is going to charge me $6.50 each, let's see how they look." (Jaimes 2018: 104)[51] Del Conde documents how she also wore Mao-style pajamas to facilitate medical exams since they were easy to roll up and down, but they were embroidered with bright red cross-stitch (Del Conde 2008: 26).

Frida's clothing was expressive and functional, and she seemed to delight in dress-up. She had worn men's clothes as a young girl and as a Communist Party sympathizer, and had been photographed wearing Chinese worker's clothes. At the same time she was very fond of nineteenth-century French couture, a love she inherited from her grandmother, whose wardrobe she preserved so she could wear the items herself (Del Conde 2008: 34).

Frida is the chosen fashion icon for the twentieth century because she was a disabled woman and a natural fashionista, embracing and using her celebrity to present her chosen self to the world. She enjoyed movies and was aware of how celebrities were posed in photographs, which is evident in images taken of her by famous fashion photographers Imogen Cunningham in 1930; Edward Weston in 1930; and Fritz Hemle (fashion photographer for Vogue) in 1943. In addition, she was a muse of sorts for the designer Elsa Schiaparelli, who was so impressed with Kahlo's eclectic style that she apparently stated that she would design an outfit "Mme Rivera style" (Del Conde 2008: 36) Frida's confidence allowed her to be portrayed openly wearing the structures that kept her body together. In 1941 she was photographed in a body cast which she had decorated with the USSR emblem (Fig. 4.8) in a nod to her ties with politics and the strength of her personal armor. Gannit Ankori explains that "She exposes her disability in her art."[52]

Figure 4.8 *Plaster corset c.1950 as displayed during the Victoria and Albert Museum's exhibition entitled "Frida Kahlo: Making Her Self Up." The plaster corset is decorated with a Soviet-era hammer-and-sickle emblem. Photo by DANIEL LEAL/ AFP via Getty Images*

Notes

1   Nielsen, K. (2013), *A Disability History of the United States*, Boston: Beacon Press.

2   See Glossary.

3   Society of Architectural Historians, (2022), *Roosevelt Warm Springs Institute for Rehabilitation*. Available online: https://sah-archipedia.org/buildings/GA-01-199-0065 (accessed December 26, 2022).

4   Ruston, R. (1977), *Dressing for disabled people*, Manchester, UK: Disabled Living Foundation.

5   Hoffman, A.M. (1979), *Clothing for the Handicapped, the Aged, and Other People with Special Needs*, Springfield, IL: Thomas Books.

6   S.H. Camp & Co., (1934), *Reference book for physicians and surgeons: The Camp system of supports for women, children, men*, Allentown, PA: Albert Drug Company.

7   Hahn, H. (1986), "Public support for rehabilitation programs: The analysis of US disability policy", *Disability, Handicap and Society*, 1 (2).

8   Nielsen, (2013), *A Disability History of the United States*, Boston, MA: Beacon Press.

9   Cardwell, V.E. (1947), *The cerebral palsied child and his care at home*, New York: Association of the Aid of Crippled Children; Dillingham, E. (1948), "Feeding and dressing techniques for the cerebral palsied child", *Crippled Child*, 26 (4), 20–2, 29.

10 Wilson Workforce and Rehabilitation Center, (2022), *Profile and History*. Available online: https://www.wwrc.virginia.gov/ProfileHistory.htm (accessed December 26, 2022).

11 Hallenbeck, P.N. (1966), "Special clothing for the handicapped: Review of research and resources", *Rehabilitation Literature*, 27 (2): 34–40.

12 Boettke, E.M. (1957), *Suggestions for physically handicapped mothers on clothing for preschool children*, Storrs, CT: University of Connecticut School of Home Economics.

13 Bare, C., Boettke, E. and Waggoner, N. (1962), *Self-Help Clothing for Handicapped Children*, Chicago, IL: National Easter Seal Society for Crippled Children and Adults/Storrs, CT: School of Home Economics, University of Connecticut.

14 Boettke Hotte, E. (1979), *Self-Help Clothing for Children who have Physical Disabilities*, (revised edition), Chicago, IL: The National Easter Seal Society for Crippled Children and Adults.

15 Scott, C. (1961), *Clothes for the Physically Handicapped Homemaker: with features suitable for all women*, (US Department of Agriculture, Home Economics Research Report No.12), Washington, DC: US Government Printing Office.

16 Sindelar, M.B. (1969), *Clothing satisfactions and preferences of physically disabled homemakers*, Master's thesis, University of Nebraska.

17 Schwab, L.O., and Sindelar, M.B. (1973), "Clothing for the physically disabled homemaker", *Rehabilitation Record*, 14: 30–40.

18 NYU Grossman School of Medicine, (2022), *About Rusk Rehabilitation*. Available online: https://med.nyu.edu/rusk/about-us/history (accessed December 26, 2022).

19 Fact sheet on Helen Cookman, New York University, Office of Information Service, October 21, 1958.

20 Cookman, H. and Zimmerman, M. (1961), *Functional Fashions for the Physically Handicapped*, New York, NY: Institute of Physical Medicine and Rehabilitation, New York University Medical Center.

21 Wright, N. (2017), "Functional Fashions for Every Child", in *Florence Eiseman, Designing Childhood for the American Century*, Museum of Wisconsin Art, West Bend, WI.

22 *Performance*, Volume XIV #6, December 1963, 12.

23 Schiro, A-M. (1995), *Vera Maxwell is dead at 93; Legendary Sportwear Designer*. Available online at: https://www.nytimes.com/1995/01/20/obituaries/vera-maxwell-is-dead-at-93-legendary-sportswear-designer.html (accessed December 26, 2022).

24 Ommerman, B. (1976), "Fashionable Clothes For Handicapped", *Central New Jersey Home News*, August 12, 1976.

25 Wright, N. (2019), Functional Fashions. Available online: https://blog.mam.org/2019/05/07/functional-fashions/ (accessed December 26, 2022).

26 Lake, S. (2016), *Bonnie Cashin: Chic is Where You Find It*, New York, NY: Rizzoli Publications International.

27 Wright, N. (2017), "Functional Fashions for Every Child", in *Florence Eiseman, Designing Childhood for the American Century*, Museum of Wisconsin Art, West Bend, WI.

28 *New York Times* (1949), *Simplicity of lines marks Cox designs*, Tuesday May 10, 30.

29 Couture Allure Vintage Fashion Blog (April 13, 2012), *Tanner of North Carolina*. Available online: http://coutureallure.blogspot.com/2012/04/tanner-of-north-carolina.html (accessed December 26, 2022).

30 Wessman, R. (1965), "Help for Handicapped: Products on Display", *Chicago Daily News*, Nov. 19.

31 Hallenbeck, P.N. (1966), "Special clothing for the handicapped: Review of research and resources", *Rehabilitation Literature*, 27(2): 34–40.

32 Email conversation with Tracey Panek, Historian at Levi Strauss & Co., 4 May 2020.

33 Natalie Wright's work represents the most consistent resource on this topic. For further information, in addition to her work already cited, please see Wright, N.E. (2002), "'Functional Fashions for the Physically Handicapped': Disability and Dress in Postwar America", *Dress*, 48 (2): 10.1080/03612112.2022.2090724, as well as her upcoming doctoral dissertation *Functional fashions: a history of clothing and disability in the United States*, University of Wisconsin-Madison.

34 Leinenweber, Inc. (1972), *What the Leinenweber Custome Tailored Wheelchair Garment Can Do for YOU*, Order form, Chicago, IL: Leinenweber, Inc.

35 J.C. Penney Company, Inc. (1961), *New Function for Clothing–Help for the Handicapped*, Fall/Winter 1961, 26–7, New York, NY: Rudolf Orthwine Corp.

36 Ibid. p. 27.

37 Hoffman, A.M. (1979), *Clothing for the Handicapped, the Aged, and Other People with Special Need*s, Springfield, IL: Thomas Books.

38 Tharp, B. J. (1964), "The Handicapped—Clothing Implications", *Clothing News and Research Findings*, University Park, PA: Cooperative Extension Service

39 Ibid.

40 Nielsen, K. (2013), *A Disability History of the United States*, Boston: Beacon Press.

41 Ibid.

42 Johnson, C.C. (1972), "Clothing for the Handicapped and Disabled", presentation at *Association of College Professors of Textiles and Clothing—Eastern Region, proceedings of the Twenty-Fifth Annual Meeting,* Washington DC, October 26 to 28, 1972.

43 Ibid.

44 Lord, J. (1970), *Clothing for the handicapped and disabled in hospital or in the community: A review of world literature 1937-1970, prepared for King Edward's Hospital Fund.* Didsbury, Manchester: The cotton silk and man-made fibres research association, Shirley Institute.

45 Macartney, P. (1973), Clothes Sense—for handicapped adults of all ages, London: Disabled Living Foundation.

46 Kahlo, F. and Zamora, M. (1995), *The letters of Frida Kahlo: cartas apasionadas*, San Francisco: Chronicle Books.

47 Del Conde, T. (2008), "Frida Kahlo: Her Look", in D. Rosenzweig and Magdalena Rosenzweig, (eds), *Self-Portrait in a Velvet Dress, Frida's Wardrobe, Fashion from the Museo Frida Kahlo*, San Francisco: CA: Chronicle Books.

48 Aragón, A.F. (2014), "Uninhabited Dresses: Frida Kahlo, from Icon of Mexico to Fashion Muse", *Fashion Theory*, 18 (5): 517–49.

49 Del Conde, T. (2008), "Frida Kahlo: Her look", in D. Rosenzweig and Magdalena Rosenzweig, (eds), *Self-Portrait in a Velvet Dress, Frida's Wardrobe, Fashion from the Museo Frida Kahlo*, San Francisco: CA: Chronicle Books.

50 Turok, M. (2008), "Frida's attire: Eclectic and ethnic", in D. Rosenzweig and Magdalena Rosenzweig, (eds), *Self-Portrait in a Velvet Dress, Frida's Wardrobe, Fashion from the Museo Frida Kahlo*, San Francisco: CA: Chronicle Books.

51 Jaimes, H. (2018), *You are always with me: Letters to Mama 1923-1932, Frida Kahlo*, edited and translated by Hector Jaimes, London: Virago.

52 Ankori, G. (2019), *In conversation: perspectives on Frida Kahlo*, Victoria and Albert Museum podcast. SoundCloud: https://soundcloud.com/vamuseum/in-conversation-perspectives-on-frida-kahlo

5

Individual Appearance Management between Two Acts: 1973–1990

Introduction

The year 1973 marks the beginning of the final "historical" phase of this journey. This year was selected because it marks the signing into law of the US Rehabilitation Act by President Richard Nixon. This federal law replaced some pre-existing laws concerning vocational rehabilitation services; expanded federal responsibilities in regards to funding research and training, and established coordination of programs within the Department of Health, Education and Welfare. The Act mandated affirmative action in hiring by the federal government and its contractors, and prohibited discrimination on the basis of disability by federal agencies, federally funded programs and federal contractors. By enabling workplace equality, the federal government of the US paved the way for accessible employment for more Americans with disabilities.

To mark the end of the chapter, the timeline closes with the passage of the Americans with Disabilities Act (ADA), which was signed into law on July 26, 1990, by President George H.W. Bush. The ADA, written to end all discrimination for disabled people and to guarantee them equal rights:

... is a federal civil rights law that prohibits discrimination against people with disabilities in everyday activities. The ADA prohibits discrimination on the basis of disability just as other civil rights laws prohibit discrimination on the basis of race, color, sex, national origin, age, and religion. The ADA guarantees that people with disabilities have the same opportunities as everyone else to enjoy employment opportunities, purchase goods and services, and participate in state and local government programs.[1]

This chapter marks an active period for government initiatives, prompted in part by the civil rights movements in the US during the 1960s and early 1970s. In 1977 the US House of Representatives' Committee on Science and Technology issued a "Report of the Panel on Research Programs to Aid the Handicapped," which called for more research into the needs of the disabled community.[2] The panel acknowledged the role that wars had played as "watersheds of awareness of the physically disabled in society," explaining how many veterans after the Civil War wore their coats with an empty sleeve to show respect for less fortunate comrades, and how prosthetic limb manufacturers were among the first industries to promote technology after the Civil War, First World War and Second World War.[3] During this time, it is worth remembering that the US was working through the post-Vietnam War era and the Veterans Administration was charged with developing rehabilitation programs for disabled veterans. This surge of interest and progress in assistance to disabled people parallels developments related to armed conflict that we have witnessed in previous chapters—the development of Lord Nelson's sun visor on his hat during the Napoleonic Wars; the Raglan sleeve developed during the Crimean War; and Howard Rusk's work in New York after the Second World War, leading to the hiring of Helen Cookman and the birth of the Functional Fashions organization. In ch.7 we will add the volunteer efforts in production of embellished fabrics and garments led by Ernest Thesiger and Annie Bindon Carter during the First World War to this list. This post-conflict sequence of events cannot be coincidental. Creativity and innovation is often born from human struggle and scarcity. There are parallels here with the dramatic innovations in Personal Protective Equipment (PPE) that were experienced during the COVID-19 pandemic.

Finally, the impact of fashion advocacy work carried out in the 1950s and 1960s by institutions, organizations and the private sector continued to gain traction during the 1970s. The goal of expanded access to employment for disabled people in the Western/industrialized world merited increased attention to the visible self in the workplace, in which fashionable clothing played a major role. This chapter will outline some of the activities during this period which focused on appearance management, self-identity and social identity.

5.1 Impact of the 1973 Rehabilitation Act

With a new law in place and a mandate for change in US government workplace programs, institutional and organizational research ramped up, resulting in an increase in the number of completed academic theses and dissertations, journal articles, workshops, classes and educational programming reflecting the interest in affordable and user-friendly fashion for disabled consumers. Rehabilitation now became a team effort, including clothing professionals, occupational therapists, rehabilitation nurses, physical therapists and counseling psychologists working together to ensure reintegration of the individual as a complete human being (Kottke 1982)[4] and to improve quality of life. Clothing was again seen as an important tool in the rehabilitation process because it facilitated the mobilization of joints and muscles, and provided practical goals in the process (Ruston 1977).[5]

The direction of research turned slightly towards reflection and evaluation of the progress in scholarship over the past decade, as well as calls for new directions for research to address the new public discourse with disability. For example, two conferences at academic institutions in the US, one held at Virginia Tech in 1976 and the other at the University of Alabama in 1977, provided forums for an interdisciplinary audience to explore not only the physical but also the psychological and social aspects of clothing and disability. Both of these universities had been instrumental in developing extension materials and teaching modules based on research, which was being carried out on and off campus. In 1975, at the 66th Annual Meeting of the American Home Economics Association in San Antonio, Texas, a Clothing and Textiles Subject Matter Session on "Clothing for the Handicapped" took place, managed by Dr. Anne Kernaleugen, a designer from the University of Alberta. The session included a talk by Kernaleugen about a display on clothing for the handicapped that was shown across Canada; a talk by Naomi Reich from the University of Arizona about lack of availability, history, and new developments in fashions for disabled consumers, and a talk by Kay Caddell from the Textile Research Center, in Lubbock, Texas.

Kay Caddell's work in Lubbock included a publication titled *Measurements, Guidelines and Solutions.*[6] In the Foreword to this publication, Caddell's contributions to the field are noted, including her research in textiles and apparel design, her background in teaching clothing design and construction at Texas Tech University, and various consulting and speaking engagements across the United States. Caddell's rationale for this book devoted to measurements is as follows: "One of the most difficult procedures in clothing the handicapped is proper fit. To achieve a desirable fit accurate measurements are necessary. Measurements can be taken in a sitting or lying position if the person is confined to a wheelchair or bed." (Caddell 1977: 1). She goes on to explain how to measure alternative postures and to describe a variety of choices for garment design. Each measurement was accompanied by a photograph for various postures (Fig. 5.1) and the book also included guidelines for solving specific fashion pattern alteration problems, accompanied by line-drawing illustrations. Caddell founded an organization, The Natural Creations, which produced garments and accessories utilizing the natural fibers of Texas, which could be purchased via catalog and mail. The designs by Caddell were produced through the Textile Research Center at Texas Tech, in cooperation with the Natural Fibers and Food Protein Commission of Texas.

Caddell's book was followed by the landmark publication, Adeline M. Hoffman's *Clothing for the Handicapped, the Aged, and Other People with Special Needs* published in 1979. This book presented the first overview of progress in the field from the 1950s, and included attention to the psychological aspects of clothing, such as personal self-worth, social stigma and societal

Figure 5.1 *Illustration reproducing a photo (original credit: Paul Fuller) from p. 13 of Kay Caddell's publication. Copy reads Leg-measure along the outside [posterior] surface of the leg from the waistline to the anklebone with the knee bent.*

acceptance.[7] Dr. Hoffman described in the Introduction how she wrote the book in response to:

> continual requests for copies of workshop proceedings, bibliographies, reference sources, and course outlines by graduate students, health department officers, Extension Service Specialists, teachers of home economics in secondary schools, colleges and universities, chain store personnel, and physically handicapped and aged individuals.
>
> HOFFMAN 1979: ix

The book covered many aspects of clothing, both physical and psychological, as well as practical solutions to problems (see Fig. 5.2) and extensive appendices.

In 1978, fashion designer Evelyn Siefert Kennedy founded the non-profit PRIDE (Promote Real Independence for the Disabled and Elderly) Foundation Inc. and in 1981, published *Dressing with Pride: Clothing Changes for Special*

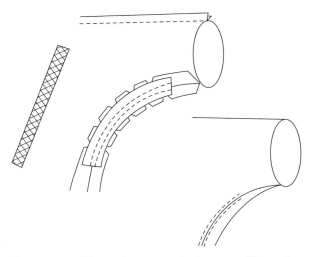

Figure 5.2 *Illustration reproducing an illustration (original credit: Lonnie M. Kennedy) from p. 65 of Adeline Hoffman's publication. Copy reads* Reinforcement of underarm seams of raglan and kimono sleeves with self-fabric cut on the bias or other matching fabric or seam binding.

Needs, a booklet that was sold by the PRIDE Foundation to raise funds.[8] The organization, based in Connecticut in the United States, was a non-profit with the primary objective of rehabilitation and independence assistance in dressing and personal grooming for the disabled and elderly. The book mentions that "available for public use is a travel trunk show of about 150 sample garments. The wardrobe includes daytime wear for home or work activities, adapted sleepwear for convalescing and special outdoor clothing for wheelchair and other needs" (p. 7), however, no evidence has been found about the whereabouts of these sample garments. Initial funds to research and prepare the book were received through a special grant from Sears, Roebuck and Co., which marks one of the few instances where we have seen mainstream retailers collaborating with a disability advocacy organization. The publication also addressed the importance of fashionable clothing; how to look at the price of goods; how to read a label and how to plan color in one's wardrobe.

The 1970s and 1980s saw an increase in university-led research focused on the specific needs of individuals with varying types of physical limitations. This resulted in published and unpublished masters and doctoral level work, which contributed to building scholarship in the field. The research began to dig deeper into specific topics than in previous decades. Segmentation of specific groups within the population allowed these groups with disabilities to be studied as focused target markets—a comparable strategy to ready-to-wear industry research practices. Children with disabilities; elderly people; homemakers; men with artificial limbs/using braces; young people with curvature of the spine and cerebral palsy were among the specific groups that were the subject of study. This type of segmentation may have been demonstrative of a growing awareness that the disabled population were not confined to one homogenous group, but consisted of subsets of smaller groups of people with varying needs and preferences, which is more in line with how the fashion industry tasks itself in addressing the needs of the abled population.[9]

Much of the research output focused primarily on product design and development, and included studies that demonstrated how to adapt patterns and clothing to accommodate specific needs; how to select clothing from ready-to-wear retailers; best practices for selection of fabrics, etc. However, some of the research began to suggest other approaches, such as targeting how clothing was used by therapists in the rehabilitation of patients and methodological approaches directly involving the user in helping to identify problems and barriers to satisfaction. Some researchers were also starting to address the lack of distribution channels for fashion for people with disabilities (Ahrbeck and Friend, 1976).[10] Researchers were discovering that the retail product selections and primary distribution options (mostly mail order) for fashion products for disabled people lacked aesthetic appeal, had poor fit and/or high cost. This research was being carried out using interviews and surveys with the disabled community, thereby implying an increase in engaging the voice of the consumer.

Many projects started to receive interest in the mainstream press. In the US commonwealth of Virginia, a newspaper article from the Alexandria Gazette on July 30, 1974, entitled "Accessible Dress" (p. 2) explains how Nancy Holloman, a Virginia Commonwealth University (VCU) assistant professor in Fashion Design, who specialized in clothing design for disabled people, made a dress for Birdie Jo Minor, who had won Miss Wheelchair Virginia and went onto the Miss Wheelchair America contest. Her dress was paid for by the VCU student chapter of the National Rehabilitation Counseling Association.

Holloman subsequently received funds from VCU to stage a fashion show to showcase designs for disabled people, and a grant from the National Endowment for the Arts (NEA) to draw sewing patterns and assemble a booklet to assist in the sewing process. Her goal at the time was to distribute the booklet widely and inexpensively.

On the other side of the commonwealth, Dr. Beatrice Kalka was developing and coordinating workshops at Virginia Polytechnic Institute & State University (Virginia Tech) designed to assist people in the surrounding community as well as university students. A March 14, 1979, *Roanoke Times* article (p. 11), entitled "Seminar to study handicap barriers", detailed a two-day seminar held at Virginia Tech which was the fourth of six regional workshops, part of a joint funded project with Virginia State University and the University of Virginia entitled "Barrier Free Environments: The Family and Community." The training was planned for professionals and public officials, and to increase public awareness of resources. Kalka's other significant contribution was an extension publication entitled "Clothes to fit your needs (for the physically limited)", publication #346–664, published by Virginia Cooperative Extension (VCE), Virginia Tech and Virginia State University, which was reprinted in April 1983. The reprint engaged Jacquelyn Yep (extension specialist in Textiles & Clothing at Iowa State University) and recommended sources of ready-made clothing. The guide included a wardrobe checksheet; attractiveness features; comfort; convenience features; fastening; safety and care of clothing. Other universities (University of Iowa, Iowa State University, University of Alabama, University of Florida, Clemson University, University of Minnesota, Michigan State University, University of Nebraska) published reports and brochures, and hosted programs and workshops targeting people who worked with disabled consumers.

5.2 Centers and Workshops

Design without Limits

Some academic efforts were so impactful that they merit their own profile. In 1977 the Design Department at Drexel University in Philadelphia started a

Fashion Design Research Studio whose objective was to study the clothing needs of physically disabled people. The idea stemmed from a presentation that Dr. M. Dolores Quinn, a professor in the Design Department at Drexel, gave at the National Conference of the Association of College Professors of Textiles and Clothing (ACPTC) in Dallas, Texas. The Fashion Design Research Studio evolved out of this presentation and Professor Quinn began to develop and teach specific courses for senior undergraduates and graduate students of fashion design.

The Fashion Design Research Studio was pioneering in a number of ways. Quinn established a collaborative design network, which included not only potential end users of the designs, but physical and occupational therapists, designers and entrepreneurs, family members and friends of disabled people, home economists, and local rehabilitation facilities. Individuals contacted the studio for assistance, and rehabilitation therapists contacted the studio to try to get copies of the clothing made for their patients. Quinn stated: "Designers and entrepreneurs became interested in potentially profitable markets. Relatives of disabled persons sought ways to answer the clothing needs of their loved ones. Home Economists continued to conduct similar research at various colleges and universities."(Quinn and Chase 1990: v)[11] The work of the program merited three NEA grants to carry out research starting in 1978. In addition, in 1982, the first National Fashion Competition for the Physically Disabled took place, under the co-sponsorship of the NEA and Drexel. Entries addressed a diverse array of disabilities.

The program elicited much press coverage, including articles in the *New York Times* as well as local news outlets. On October 31, 1979, *The Washington Star* ran a feature on "Possibilities Unlimited," which reported how the NEA had awarded "$15,000 to Nesbitt College of Drexel University, for Clothing Designed Especially for The Handicapped," with matching funds from the Samuel S. Fels Fund; the William Penn Foundation; a local chapter of the Ladies Garment Workers' Union (LGWU), William J. Netsky of Ship-N-Shore and the Sun Company. The article also reported how Professor Quinn consulted with the Moss Rehabilitation Center in Philadelphia and with Muriel Zimmerman (Helen Cookman's original partner), hoping to put clothing into production. In the article, photos show a fashion shoot using clothing supplied by local Philadelphia stores, including Woodward & Lothrop and Garfinckel's. Brands included a sweater by Claude Barthelemy, pants by Parallel, a button front coat-dress by Evan Picone, a wool jacket by Anne Klein, and separates by Calvin Klein. This is one of the first cases where we see a fashion spread in the media utilizing available fashion from brick and mortar retailers while focusing on the disabled consumer.

The Fashion Research team realized the diversity and potential of their work, so the next step was to focus on publishing a book about practical fashion options for wheelchair users, crutch users, prosthetic users and people with limited mobility.[12] *Design without Limits* was published in 1990, with the purpose of showing that clothing "can be as stylish, sophisticated, and current as the work done by any 'Seventh Avenue' designer" (Quinn and Chase 1990: vi). They also wanted to provide information to allow designers, dressmakers, and tailors to address problems in a practical way. The Simplicity Pattern Company, which in 1987 had put out a leaflet entitled "Sewing for the Handicapped," assisted in the publication. The book was illustrated by Steven Stipelman, a renowned fashion illustrator, and Catherine Clayton Purnell.

Contents of the book covered every aspect of design and construction for clothing. Quinn opened the book by discussing how it evolved, and how her design approach could be broken down into the difference between a seated posture and a standing posture. Following this introduction, there was a section on resources: sewing and material supplies, lists of cooperative extensions organizations and foundations, special aids and clothing for disabled people, and clothing catalogs. Quinn's discussion continued with insight into the psychological impact of clothing, design considerations, fashion awareness, technical skills of fabric knowledge, patternmaking and construction, plus input from the wearer, physical and occupational therapists, and medical staff. An illustrated section showed a "Portfolio" of styles, with color examples (Fig. 5.3). The book contained chapters on how to make adaptations for the seated figure, the standing figure, and those with limited dexterity; plus information on how to take measurements, alter patterns, select appropriate fabrics, and a reading list.

Figure 5.3 *Page from* Design without Limits, *with illustration by Steven Stipelman.* *Courtesy of Steven Stipelman*

Quinn's philosophy as stated in the foreword of the *Design without Limits* book is as follows:

> I believe that clothing is an art form and therefore must always be constructed out of wonderful materials, must be imaginatively and finely crafted so that it may be applied to the body and removed with comfort and ease. Clothing must enhance and fit the human form both when the body is static and when it is in motion. Clothing must always support the body, and while it is subordinate to the person wearing it, clothing must in itself be visually beautiful and contribute to the beauty of the wearer.
>
> QUINN and CHASE 1990: viii[13]

Many acknowledgments are paid in the opening of the book to the forerunners of Quinn's efforts in design, including: Bonnie Cashin, Joanne Boles, Kay Caddel, Adeline Hoffman, Audrey Newton, Naomi Reich and Muriel Zimmerman. The book remains one of the most comprehensive guides to design and construction for what is now known as adaptive clothing. This focus on design from the start marks a transition towards emphasizing the aesthetic consideration as well as functionality, which had been Helen Cookman's mission with her Functional Fashions label. Quinn states "Adaptive clothing is not with fashion as a priority; it is designed only with the disability in mind. The integration of all the elements necessary for a complete design has not been achieved in most adaptive clothing," (Quinn and Chase 1990: 5). The book is the first of its kind to include the practical use of design principles, such as using line, shape, color, and texture. Further to that, the authors explain how to create illusion on the disabled body. This also marks one of the first times that we see a guide that uses all the elements and principles of design in clothing for disabled people, rather than just focusing on the purely technical.

Assessing the impact of *Design without Limits*, I believe it is safe to say that Quinn's contribution of the combined program at Drexel and resulting book is in line with the impact of the Functional Fashions label in evolving the field. Even though *Design without Limits* was not a retail brand or place for designers to collaborate and sell products, focus on the power of tools already at the fashion designer's disposal and how to use them for the disabled consumer is a significant contribution. The comprehensive nature of the program, plus the funding and support that Quinn was able to achieve during the active years of the program, represent a shift and perhaps a turning point in how seriously these efforts at integration should be taken within the fashion industry.

Center for Universal Design

While not focused on fashion, Ronald Mace's contribution to the design of built environments and products that benefit people of all abilities deserves to be mentioned here. Mace, an established architect whose activism had contributed to national legislation aimed at ending discrimination against disabled people, established the Center for Accessible Housing in 1989, which became known worldwide as the Center for Universal Design at North Carolina State University. The Principles of Universal Design as promoted by the Center were written for the built environment, but can be applied as much to clothing as to other products and environments, since they provide guideposts and checkpoints that ensure products and services are as inclusive as possible. These seven guiding principles for the design of products and services are to ensure for: (1) Equitable Use; (2) Flexible Use; (3) Simple and Intuitive Use; (4) Perceptible Information; (5) Tolerance for Error; (6) Low Physical Effort; and (7) Size and Space for Approach and Use (see Fig. 5.4). I believe that these principles can be incorporated fully into clothing design and that Universal Design provides a stable and inclusive framework within which to design for all body types and abilities. The Center for Universal Design is still housed within the College of Design at NC State in Raleigh, North Carolina.[14]

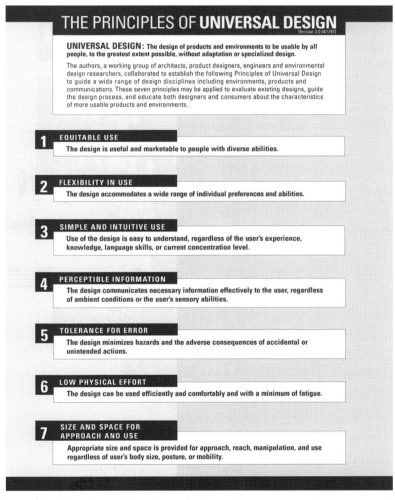

Figure 5.4 *The Seven Principles of Universal Design, as established by the Center of Universal Design, College of Design, North Carolina State University. Copyright 1997 NC State University, The Center for Universal Design*

5.3 Other Relevant Publications

Academic research during this time began to address processes as well as specific product-related issues. One result of this was Shannon and Reich's landmark study which established basic guidelines to match specific physical limitations with clothing related needs.[15] In addition, the social and psychological aspects of fashion's relationship with disability grew in importance throughout the 1980s. For example, studies were carried out examining the impact of dress in the evaluation of disabled job applicants; the types of disability cues in functional clothing; and the importance of clothing in independent living. Lamb studied the information and communication gaps regarding clothing availability and found that disabled consumers preferred to receive information in the form of printed materials over any other method.[16] This shift towards the psychological and consumer science aspects of fashion helped promote the social acceptance of disabled people having equal access to the industry, but still there was little movement in the retail arena, either in product offerings, accessibility or marketing. All researchers acknowledged that useful and usable information must make its way to the consumer as well as the academic community, but the impetus to make good on this recommendation was not forthcoming from the fashion industry.

Towards the end of the 1970s and on into the 1980s, the state of the scholarship in some areas was sufficiently advanced so that bibliographies and summaries could be written. In 1982, Sandra S. Hutton, at the University of Nebraska-Lincoln, published a database on the Clothing Needs of the Handicapped and Elderly.[17] Hutton explains in the acknowledgements that the report was part of a larger study in which she planned a computerized database of clothing periodical literature. The report covered literature published between January 1970 to December 1981 and contained references and abstracts of 179 citations found in the published literature. Hutton also mentions that the Clothing Database contained "citations and abstracts of 5252 published articles on clothing and related issues" (Hutton 1982: Acknowledgments).

Commercial and community organizations continued collaborations with researchers to form partnerships resulting in publications and publicity. The National Easter Seal Society co-sponsored the book *Self-Help Clothing for Children who have Physical Disabilities* with Eleanor Boettke Hotte, who was

Professor Emeritus at the University of Connecticut School of Home Economics and Family Studies.[18] Boettke had pioneered the development of self-help clothing for children and their parents in the late 1950s, in order to help mothers with dexterity challenges by promoting dressing independence for their children. Boettke writes in the Introduction to the 1979 publication about the progress that she had seen over twenty years of research.

> The revision required a review of the present clothing picture—of what is available, what is being worn, and the changing attitudes that society has about clothing. Consideration had to be given to the greater ability that individuals with disabilities have today to participate in events and happenings around them. The barriers are beginning to break down and, as they do, independence has a greater reward.
>
> BOETTKE HOTTKE, 1979: Foreword

Collaborative efforts with aspects of the fashion industry continued. Talon/Velcro Company's Consumer Education Division published a booklet entitled "Convenience Clothing and Closures" during the 1970s. The publication was supported by USDA Cooperative Extension Association and NYU Medical Center Institute of Rehabilitation Medicine. It contained general clothing selection considerations; a chart of common disabilities and solutions (not just fastenings); easy-to-manage closures, with emphasis on different types of Talon Zippers and Velcro fastenings, and adaptations using Velcro and zippers.

The Sister Kenny Institute in Minneapolis, MN, published Rehabilitation Publication 737, "Clothing for the Handicapped: Fashion Adaptations for Adults and Children." The Institute received help from Textile and Clothing Specialists at the University of Minnesota, and the publication was made possible in part by a grant from the Fashion Group of General Mills, Inc. It offered potential solutions to problem areas, as well as patterns for adaptation to commercial patterns such as Kwik Sew, Butterick, Stretch and Sew, Vogue, and Simplicity. Simplicity had a history of being involved with adaptive clothing since the 1950s.

Despite all these efforts, the face of fashion retail for the disabled consumer appeared to remain somewhat stagnant; however, there were efforts underway which gave some insight into the opening up of the retail market in the early twenty-first century.

5.4 The Beginning Role of Retail

Small businesses that were owned and operated by people with disabilities and their family members had been the norm in most commercial startup ventures up to this point. They continued to be the primary way that the disabled population could gain access to items at the consumer level during this period. However, during the 1970s, startup companies and available products were increasing in variety. The business models were extremely varied. "Ventura Carrying Aids" sold fourteen options of bags in eight fabric choices available by mail order, which was interesting, since fashionable accessories had not previously been given much coverage. "Fashions Handee for You," a custom garment and Sew-it-Yourself kit company based in Lowville, NY, created designs and ready-to-sew kits for disabled women, which were sold through mail-order catalogs with illustrations. The Sew-it-Yourself kit contained fabric which had been pre-cut for a garment, with Velcro and all necessary fastenings, easy-to-follow directions and diagrams to help the consumer complete construction. The company provided the cut fabric because "cutting out a garment may present a real problem to many." Prices ranged from $3.00 to $32.00.

On the Rise/I can do it Myself, based out of Eugene, OR, was started by Mary Harless whose daughter Melissa had cerebral palsy. This company sold customized garments made from cotton calico fabrics in different color options.[19] Styles included a girls' front-wrap dress, pants, reversible jacket, shirts and tops, ponchos, overalls, all with decorative appliqués. Adult styles included a ladies' robe, a skirt, bathing suit, pair of mittens, pair of pants, a dress, a blouse, a housedress, a cape, a nightgown, men's shirts, pants, jackets, tote bag, and foot warmers.

PTL Designs Inc: Apparel Manufacturing for the Elderly and Physically Handicapped, was based in Stillwater OK and founded in 1975 by Mary Murphy, Ann Simms and Phyllis Jo Acuff. This was a direct mail, apparel manufacturing operation, focused on custom production to meet the psychological as well as physical needs of the individual. The company was founded as a cottage industry style of production, using a bundled outwork system, and provided work for local seamstresses. Multiple styles for men, women and children were sold through a catalog system, which included price, size and fabric list. Chapter 7 of this book which focuses on disabled makers and designers goes into more detail regarding the context of entrepreneurship and adaptive fashion.

Established retail companies such as Hart Schaffner & Marx also became involved in this space, going so far as to survey their disabled customers' fashion preferences, with findings which shed light on preferred fabric types (smooth and permanent press); preferred waistband types, and the difficulty of shopping. Some other specialized retailers who began or grew during this period include the following, some of which are still active at the time of writing:

- Abilitywear

- Adaptogs

- Adrian's Closet

- American Health Care Apparel Ltd.

- Anitavee's Adaptive Apparel

- Forde's Functional Fashions, Inc.

- JC Penney Easy Dressing Line/Catalog Division

- MEE Too! Clothing Ltd.

- Professional Fit Clothing

- Rolli-Moden

- Silverts

- Specially for You

- Wardrobe Wagon

These retailers mark a transition from the family-led ventures of the 1950s, 1960s and 1970s towards a new, perhaps more sophisticated operation where the needs of the disabled consumer were being met in a number of different ways, but more importantly, the disabled consumer market was being recognized as having spending power but not enough products available for their money to be spent on. Very few mainstream retailers, however, appeared in this mix.

Summary

- This chapter has documented the growth in interest and research that occurred after the US Rehabilitation Act was passed in 1973, much of it as a result of increased government funding, but some of it a result of the urgency of a post-war period (in the United States) where veterans were once again directly in the public eye. Much of this work translated into new academic programs and design studios; workshops and centers, plus a huge increase in scholarly writing and dissemination of work being completed in the academy

- The growing momentum also saw a shift in the merchandise mix for the retail industry, not towards high fashion, but at least to products that were designed through listening to the consumer and collecting feedback

- The global fashion industry was still reluctant to move forward on marketing, product design and development, manufacturing and distribution for the disabled community. The next chapter will show how the ADA and the internet finally propelled the mainstream fashion community towards inclusion.

Profile: *Sunae Park Evans, Senior Costume Conservator, Smithsonian Institution*

During this period, more museums started to actively collect and display fashion as an artistic category of products. I chatted with a costume specialist at the Smithsonian Institution in Washington DC about her work and whether she had witnessed any intersectionality between fashionable dress and disability during her tenure.

Author: What do you do at the Smithsonian, and how long have you been there?

Dr. Park Evans: My title is senior costume conservator and I started working at the American History Museum in 1999. At that time I had been working in the Natural History Museum for about five years, which was a little different, but a big help as experience. I was working with ethnographic history but I had done an internship before that, which led me to where I am today. So now I work on any costume or textile materials objects in the American History [division] and we prepare them for exhibition, for rehousing or care.

Author: How have museums handled fashion objects and accessories that have been worn and adapted for people with disabilities? Have you come across many items that have been worn by someone with a disability? And how do you identify them?

Dr. Park Evans: I've not really seen many objects related to accessibility and fashion, but I have worked with sportswear for the Adaptive Sports exhibition ["Everyone Plays!" exhibit, October 1, 2016 to March 26, 2017, Museum of American History]. I was specifically working with the Mike Schultz exhibit [for the Special Olympics].

Author: Do you think there are challenges preventing more adaptive fashion from being shown and curated?

Dr. Park Evans: I don't think so, because our museum designers and curators are willing to work together and we are all happy to do it. But not many objects are really available for curators to collect. We have a collections planning team and they have to include all different kinds of collections. They cannot just focus on one category of objects. The curators have their research-focused areas. So that all has to go together.

Author: Have you found anything that has been adapted to fit, like padding?

Dr. Park Evans: Well, the eighteenth century is really challenging because the body shape is so different from today. It all has to do with the culture and the fashion. As an example, for men's eighteenth-century breeches, they were really tight on the body. When I was working with George Washington's uniform, it had been on display for more than 100 years because everybody [visitors to American History] has to be able to see that uniform. So because of that, the surface was damaged because they didn't really properly mount it on the mannequin; it has many wrinkles, so when you see the front part, it's very wrinkled. Then there was damage, because they didn't know exactly how to mount it on the fiberglass mannequin, it was very hard to make this historical shape. We had an exhibition about the presidency in 1999. That was my first job when I came to the museum and I brought in new mannequins that are made of ethafoam to enable us to change the shapes. I also suggested not having a face and hands. When people come to the museum, I want them to really concentrate on the object.

Author: Have any First Ladies had any kind of disability?

Dr. Park Evans: I never thought about that or about adaptation. When I make the form, I make the pattern for it so it should be exactly the same as the body, but sometimes it isn't, so I have to change the forms, and I always thought that perhaps it wasn't a well-made object, or costume. From now on I will look into it because I never thought about it. It would be interesting to go back and look. We have a First Ladies collection, we could look back and we could trace a person, to see if there were any changes or differences. It would be so exciting to find out that way.

Author: If you come across anything else, please let me know!

Dr. Park Evans: Actually, there is one more object—I was working with Ray Charles' [blind American musician] costumes, and his former manager came to the lab and he told me how he had embroidered RC on his socks and on the shirt cuff so Ray knew which side out to wear the garment by figuring it out for himself.

Figure 5.5 *Ray Charles' performance suit, showing his initials embroidered on his left cuff. Courtesy Division of Cultural and Community Life, National Museum of American History, Smithsonian Institution*

Notes

1   ADA.gov. (2022), *Introduction to the Americans with Disabilities Act*. Available online: https://www.ada.gov/ada_intro.htm (accessed December 26, 2022).

2   US House of Representatives Committee on Science & Technology. (1977), *"Report of the panel on research programs to aid the handicapped"*, Washington DC: US Government Printing Office.

3   Ibid. p. 30.

4   Kottke, F. J. (1982), "Philosophic considerations of quality of life for the disabled", *Archives of Physicians Medical Rehabilitation*, 63 (2): 60–2.

5   Ruston, R. (1977), *Dressing for disabled people: A manual for nurses and others,* London: Disabled Living Foundation.

6   Caddell, K. (1977), *Measurements, Guidelines and Solutions*, Lubbock, TX: Vintage Press.

7   Hoffman, A.M. (1979), *Clothing for the Handicapped, the Aged, and Other People with Special Needs*, Springfield, IL: Thomas Books.

8   Kennedy, E.S. (1981), *Dressing with Pride: Clothing Changes for Special Needs,* Groton, CT: PRIDE Foundation, Inc.

9   These groups and the full reference for these research studies can be found in S. Hutton's bibliography referenced at the end of this chapter and U. Chowdhary's, referenced in ch. 6.

10 Ahrbeck, E. and Friend, S. (1976), "Clothing—An Asset or Liability? Designing for Specialized Needs", *Rehabilitation Literature*, 37 (10): 295–6.

11 Quinn, M.D. and Chase, R.W. (1990), *Design without Limits: Designing and Sewing for Special Needs*, Philadelphia, PA: Drexel Design Press and New York, NY: Simplicity Pattern Co. Inc.

12 Ibid.

13 Ibid.

14 North Carolina State University College of Design (2022). *Center for Universal Design*. Available online: https://design.ncsu.edu/research/center-for-universal-design/ (accessed December 26, 2022).

15 Shannon, E. and Reich, N. (1979). "Clothing and Related Needs of Physically Handicapped Persons", *Rehabilitation Literature*, 40 (1).

16 Lamb, J.M. (1984). "Family use of functional clothing for children with physical disabilities". *Rehabilitation Literature*, 45 (5–6), 146–50.

17 Hutton, S.S. (1982), *Index to Periodical Articles and Clothing Database Contents Dealing with the Clothing Needs of the Handicapped and Elderly*, Departmental Report #23, University of Nebraska-Lincoln

18 Boettke Hotte, E. (1979), *Self-Help Clothing for Children who have Physical Disabilities*, (revised edition), Chicago, IL: The National Easter Seal Society for Crippled Children and Adults.

19 See Glossary.

6

Contemporary Design and Technology

Introduction

This chapter looks at the changes that have taken place in the fashion industry since the 1990 Americans with Disabilities Act (ADA). The ADA is not the only policy decision to have been made to further the rights of disabled people; the UK Disability Discrimination Act was passed in 1995, and the UN Convention on the Rights of Persons with Disabilities (UNCRPD) was established in 2011. There is no direct evidence that these decisions had an impact on the intersection between fashion and disability, but their impact on the rights of disabled people in general may have increased awareness and understanding of global rights to accessibility and affordability of products and services.

This chapter will consider how the design community has addressed the creation of products for people with disabilities in contemporary times, beginning with a high-level view of what is happening in the mass-market retail sector, and then following up with some conversations with individuals about what design for disability means in today's world, using face-to-face interviews with professionals in different aspects of the industry. Some thoughts about a need for a design process for fashion and disability are introduced and the chapter concludes with a look at current and future design opportunities, some of which revolve around technology.

6.1 The Americans with Disabilities Act

On July 26, 1990, US President George H.W. Bush signed the Americans with Disabilities Act into law. The ADA was revised in 2010 and again in 2016 and has become integral to creating equal opportunities for the disabled community in the United States. The ADA defines disability as a "physical or mental impairment that substantially limits one or more major life activities, a person who has a history or record of such an impairment, or a person who is perceived by others as having such an impairment."[1] By not naming specific impairments, the ADA allows for flexibility of interpretation, which may or may not work in favor of the disabled person.

The language as written called for the removal of barriers in many specific aspects of public life: Employment, Public Transportation, Accommodation, and Communications, as well as enacting other large-scale Equal Opportunity provisions. While fashion is not named specifically, there are several places in the ADA where the interpretation of the language indirectly includes shopping and self-care as areas of equal opportunity. In the section regarding Public Accommodations, for example, a clothing store is included in the definition. In addition, one aspect of Major Life Activity is stated as "caring for oneself," therefore one could interpret the acquisition of accessible and appropriate clothing and accessories as integral to self-care.

Other sections of the Act allude directly to provisions for accessible products and their acquisition. In recognition that a greater percentage of Americans with disabilities were entering the workforce at the time the Act was being written, dress codes were included in the original ADA language. Typically, when dress codes are established, they either require the wearing of specific items of clothing and/or accessories, or prohibit them. According to the ADA, if someone with a disability requests a clothing modification as a reasonable accommodation, the employer must consider the modification unless a dress code is required as part of the job.

In the section of the ADA regarding Public Accommodations and Commercial Facilities (Title III) there is more language directly pertaining to access to clothing. Section 36.307 (Accessible or Special Goods) states that:

The rule does not require a public accommodation to alter its inventory to include accessible or special goods with accessibility features that are designed for, or facilitate use by, individuals with disabilities . . . accessible or special goods include such items as . . . special sizes or lines of clothing . . . Although a public accommodation is not required . . . to modify its inventory, it is required by Sec.36.307(b), at the request of an individual with disabilities, to order accessible or special goods that it does not customarily maintain in stock if, in the normal course of its operation, it makes special orders for unstocked goods, and if the accessible or special goods can be obtained from a supplier with whom the public accommodation customarily does business. For example, a clothing store would be required to order specially-sized clothing at the request of an individual with a disability, if it customarily makes special orders for clothing that it does not keep in stock, and if the clothing can be obtained from one of the store's customary suppliers.[2]

In the Accessible Design guidelines, the accessibility of retail fitting rooms is mentioned. The guidelines state that 5 percent or at least one room shall comply with the following: "Regardless of the type of facility, dressing, fitting, and locker rooms should provide people with disabilities rooms that are equally private and convenient to those provided others."[3] Additional design guidelines include language on accessible storage of clothing, and on the height and operational parts of washing machines in public use.

What is offered to begin this chapter is that with the passage of the ADA in 1990, attention appears to have been given to the processes of acquiring and using fashion items. At first glance the Act appears not directly applicable to the fashion industry, but its language can be interpreted as providing equal access to self-care, assistive devices, workplace dress code modifications, potential access to "special sizes or lines of clothing," accessible fitting rooms and the ability to care for one's clothing. These items are contextual, but I feel that it is important to point out that they were included in the language of this important piece of legislation.

In the UK, the Disability Discrimination Act of 1995 (revised 2005 and replaced by the Equality Act of 2010) also banned discrimination in "access to goods, facilities, and services."[4] Worldwide, the UNCRPD was adopted in

2006, with all EU Member States at the time signing the convention. The UNCRPD is "the first comprehensive human rights treaty of the 21st century."[5] It has eight priority areas, including Accessibility, defined as "make goods and services accessible to people with disabilities and promote the market of assistive devices." In the European Union, the UNCRPD entered into force in 2011, with all EU Member States signing on to the Convention.[6] All these agreements, which cover global and regional legislation, allow for the provision of equal access to goods and services for disabled people, in which case I argue that fashion can be considered both **goods** and a **service**.

6.2 Fashion Design Developments in Context

Previous chapters have demonstrated that design for disabled consumers has existed, certainly as far back as the Renaissance and perhaps further, but the design process was more akin to product engineering and problem-solving than the creation of new aesthetic directions. The individual makers whose job it was to "bestow a good shape where Nature has not designed it," in the words of Campbell (1747) went largely unnoticed and unacknowledged.[7] Their ingenuity and creativity in changing the shape of garments to fit bodies was wrapped into the natural expectation that their dressmaking and tailoring skills would get the job done without extra requirements. Over the years, the development of Western/industrialized fashion, in moving away from the power of the individual craftsman to fit a specific body and towards a "few-sizes-fits-all" system that comprises the modern ready-to-wear industry, has diminished the ability to not only fit, but Design (capital D intentional) for individuality of the body. Furthermore, the creation of artificial fashion shapes over the years since the 1700s that were not necessarily based on the human form and its need for comfort, served to create a system that in itself was exclusive. This made the job of the dressmaker/tailor increasingly difficult when trying to "disguise" disabled bodies and/or create accessibility, in addition to creating fashion silhouettes for bodies that did not conform to the prevailing fashion tastes. The wrapping, draping and fastening of geometric shapes of fabric that has persisted in many other global cultures over centuries is by nature a more flexible, accessible, and inclusive practice, and one which we see returning in the current "gender-neutral" global fashion trend, although it remains to be seen how much this trend will impact high-street, mass market retail.

Traditional fashion history has focused on stylistic changes over the decades or "periods," with most attention being concentrated on the European monarchy, aristocracy, and fashionable elite, whose social circles appeared to be responsible for creating and morphing styles in almost mercurial ways. This design of shape and detail was facilitated by nameless tailors, dressmakers, mantua-makers, milliners, and various other skilled craftspeople, whose job was to transform the movers and shakers of society into embodied representations of power via the latest styles, female examples of which from the nineteenth century can be seen in Figs 6.1 a and b.

History also shows how politics, war, and economics impacted design changes through exchange of styles, artistic convention, trade and the manufacture of materials. Prior to Charles Frederick Worth, known to many as the "Father of

Figures 6.1 a and b *Examples of changes in silhouette between (a) early and (b) mid-nineteenth century women's fashions. a. Photo by The Print Collector/Heritage Images via Getty Images; b. Photo by Culture Club/Getty Images*

Haute Couture," and most definitely a "designer of styles," there is little discussion of *how* fashion was designed and *who* was responsible for bringing these stylistic changes to life. With the exception of Rose Bertin, dressmaker to Marie Antoinette, there is little information about how changes in style were crafted and who was technically and artistically responsible for the first change in sleeve length, dip in neckline, height of collar, etc.—the small yet powerful changes in detail that typically signify a change in direction for the fashion of the times.

With so little public information available about all but the most notorious couturiers and designers after the age of Worth, there was certainly no known initiative in fashion design that took the needs of disabled people into consideration in a proactive, rather than reactive, manner until the mid-twentieth century. Helen Cookman's Functional Fashions was in itself a product of the times, both in terms of its mark on the styles of the period and its activism. The 1950s, as previously mentioned, can be seen historically as the genesis of American Style, with relaxed silhouettes primed for a public in need of a simpler, more convenient and less formal lifestyle. The designers who worked with Cookman within the Functional Fashions label picked up the baton of the scores of nameless tailors, dressmakers, mantua-makers, and other craftspeople who had relied on their creative ingenuity to solve the design problems of the past. Bonnie Cashin's dog leash skirt, described in ch. 4, with its use of ingenious fasteners to assist wheelchair users parallels William of Orange's adapted waistcoat, discussed in ch. 2, which was hastily opened up and re-fastened with functional yet decorative bows. Both were born from user-based necessity, and both evolved into completely novel approaches which married decorative fastenings and a fashionable aesthetic with the functionality of access.

The body of design work from the 1960s until the 1990s focused on functional needs assessment, primarily for individualized situations. The idea of marrying fashion and innovation together with functionality took somewhat of a back seat to making sure that users' functional needs were met first and foremost, which is in itself a necessary part of the process. In contemporary times, we have witnessed designers such as Izzy Camilleri, Lucy Jones, and Grace Jun playing an instrumental part in bringing the fashion aesthetic back into design for the disabled consumer, continuing the intention of Helen Cookman's initiative with Functional Fashions in the 1960s and Delores' Quinn's *Design without Limits* in the 1970s and 1980s. These contemporary designers will be revisited a little later in the chapter, but first it is necessary to take a high-level overview of what is happening in the contemporary mass market in order to see how things have changed over the past twenty or so years.

One of the first mainstream retailers in the US to start producing and marketing adaptive clothing was the discount retailer Target. Target's initiative began in childrenswear with Stacey Monsen, a designer on the product development and design team, and mother to a child with autism. Stacey's ideas went into the creation of the line Cat & Jack™, launched online in October 2017, with forty different styles in sizes 2T to 5T for toddlers and XS–XXL for kids. Target engaged the voice of their customer by gathering input from end-use consumers and soliciting input from organizations who work with disabled children. The current properties of Cat & Jack™ clothing are that the items have no tags or seams; bodysuits have easy access for diaper changing, wheelchair-friendly jackets have side-openings and zip-on sleeves, and clothing has hidden openings for abdominal access. Fig. 6.2 shows an example of a garment from the Target video "Future at Heart: Cat and Jack Adaptive" which describes some of the design and development decisions that go into

Figure 6.2 *Cat & Jack™ Adaptive kids' jeans, showing an added opening on the side for accessibility. Stills from "Future at Heart: Cat and Jack Adaptive," September 14, 2018. Courtesy of Target Press Center. © 2023 Target Brands, Inc. Target, the Bullseye Design and Bullseye Dog are trademarks of Target Brands, Inc. All rights reserved*

the line.[8] In this case, the zipper opening has been placed on the sides of a pair of jeans to facilitate the donning and doffing processes.

Fig. 6.3 shows a child's shirt that is being developed to have hidden accessible openings for children who need abdominal access.[9] The prices are in line with other Target private label brands and comparable to items at other discount retailers at the time of writing.[10]

Target's adult offerings include adaptive belts in the men's Goodfellow & Co™ line, which is advertised for one-handed users; women's adaptive boot-cut jeans in the Universal Thread™ line, advertised as having flat seams, no back pocket, wide waistband, and side zippers for donning and doffing; men's long and short sleeve T-shirts with flat seams, no tags, and a long curved hem at lower back; men's boot-cut jeans with an adjustable waistband and zippers at the hem; men's joggers, men's chinos, a woman's denim jacket, an adaptive sweatshirt, a crewneck sweatshirt with back buttons and holes in the cuffs through which thumbs can be placed, to name but a few. Searching the website is facilitated by selecting Adaptive Feature as a search term with categories such as Wheelchair Friendly, Sensory Friendly and Ease of Dressing to choose from. All adult adaptive wear listed prices are comparable to other items in the

Figure 6.3 *Detail of Cat & Jack™ shirt, showing abdominal accessibility. Stills from "Future at Heart: Cat and Jack Adaptive," September 14, 2018. Courtesy of Target Press Center. © 2023 Target Brands, Inc. Target, the Bullseye Design and Bullseye Dog are trademarks of Target Brands, Inc. All rights reserved*

same line. As the adaptive women's wear Target brand, Universal Thread was rolled out in 2018, just after Cat & Jack, to "fit individuals of all shapes and sizes." Universal Thread's adaptive features include tag-free, flat seams, extra soft materials, high-rise backs and longer inseams, wider leg bottoms, no back pockets, and faux front pockets. The entire line is priced below $50.00, and at time of writing, Universal Thread items are available online and in stores.

Possibly the most well-known retail brand to address the needs of the adaptive market in the US is Tommy Hilfiger with the Tommy Adaptive lines for children and adults, launched in 2016 for children and 2017 for adults. Tommy Hilfiger himself has children on the autistic spectrum and his sister had Multiple Sclerosis. Tommy Adaptive clothing uses manageable closures and the brand pushed to have "the same design as our mainstream collection but add innovative modifications and make dress easier." The Hilfiger brand also used input and feedback from consumers. The website explains how Hilfiger embraces everyone affected by a disabled individual's needs: "American cool style with innovative design twists that make getting dressed easier for the entire family." The website is designed to shop by category such as Easy Closures, Fits for Prosthetics, Comfort and Seated Wear, Port Accessible, Ease of Dressing, and Wheelchair Friendly categories. Easy Closures includes magnetic buttons, Velcro™, "one-handed" magnetic zippers, port openings, pull up loops, side seam openings, and center back openings on shirts.

Another retailer with a substantial online presence in the consumer fashion market is Zappos with its Zappos Adaptive website, which markets accessories, medical wear, easy on/off sandals, intimates and underwear, Runway of Dreams looks and wider-fit shoes. Zappos' website tag is "Functional and Fashionable Products to Make Life Easier." On the Zappos website one can find well-known fashion brands such as UGG Universal, SOREL Easy On/Off Shoes, Reebok, Crocs Footwear, and Steve Madden Easy On shoes. The UGG promo video features a wide selection of disabled people showing how the products were developed based on consumer feedback. The Runway of Dreams Collection shows looks on the runway on a model and then how to shop each look next to the runway photo, making it very easy to obtain access to "looks" seen on the runway.

Zappos Adaptive also offers an Intimates page, consisting of a curated collection of lines such as CRISSCROSS Intimates, Slick Chicks, Under

Armour seamless, Silverts, Anita and InstantRecoveryMD mastectomy and surgical procedure bras. Zappos offers an accessories page, selling Hickies no-tie laces, ostomy covers in varying colors and fabrics, PortaPocket belts and accessories, and many other options. This product assortment makes Zappos Adaptive a one-stop shop for adaptive fashion.

The athletic wear company Nike developed shoes in 2015 that were marketed as "Easy On Easy Go." Now known as the FlyEase shoes, they are marketed as having "technology developed from insights from the disability community" and in marketing imagery the shoe is shown on a variety of bodies. The word Adaptive is not used anywhere in the marketing. There are multiple variations of FlyEase shoes, including the Metcon, a training shoe with a flexible heel that "snaps back into shape" and Velcro straps. As an example of Universal Design, the FlyEase addresses many of the principles laid out in ch. 5, so that equitable use is achieved because of the easier donning and doffing process for people lacking mobility in their feet and ankles. In 2021

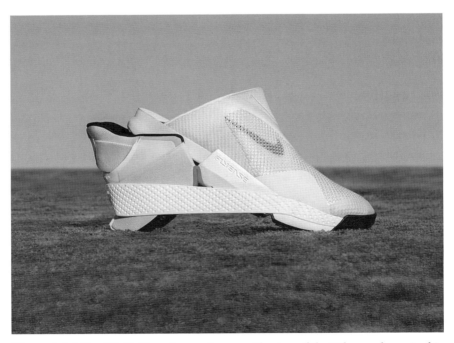

Figure 6.4 *Nike GO FlyEase. Image shows a side view of the Nike sneaker raised in the articulated position for easy donning. Photo Credit: Nike.com*

Nike launched the hands-free GO FlyEase trainer. This shoe does not require hands to put in on or take it off, since the design allows the foot to slip into it and then the shoe closes around the foot using a midsole hinge built into the shoe. US Paralympic athlete Sarah Reinersten explains: "We designed this based on human behaviour," . . . "So we feel like this is intuitive in the way that your foot goes into a shoe–you can step in and go." . . . "This is one of the most universal shoes ever," said Reinersten. "This is a solution for so many people. This is for everybody."[11]

Some contemporary companies extend beyond the products to create community. One of these is SpecialKids.com, founded in 2013 by Sasha Radwan who wanted to bring the stories of special needs children out into the open and provide products for them and their families. The items are age appropriate, stylish and the company has a large merchandise assortment, including both clothing and accessories. Based in the UK, the company has an online community, and includes blogs and interviews on its webpage.

In the accessories arena, Lucy Jones' company, FFORA, whose tagline is "Designed to be Seen," provides unique and graceful wheelchair accessories such as the "Essential Bag," which can be worn and carried in a variety of ways; bottles and holders and a wheelchair attachment system, which is described as the "heart of the FFORA product range" and the "building block to the FFORA assortment of wheelchair-attachable accessories." FFORA has elevated wheelchair-accessible products into the zone of luxury. Lucy's story in her own words is included further along in this chapter.

ALLELES, a Canadian design and manufacturing company, began making prosthetic covers in 2013. Their covers are custom fitted for each client, and come in a wide array of fun and fashionable designs and colors, available under categories such as Fantasy, Geometric and Robotic. Co-founder McCauley Wanner's focus is to "come up with a fashion forward way for amputees to express themselves through their prosthesis."[12]

This section of the chapter addressing recent developments must include a mention of the impact of Runway of Dreams on modern fashion and disability. The founder of Runway of Dreams, Mindy Scheier—herself a trained fashion designer—was prompted to start solving the problems experienced by her own son Oliver, who has Muscular Dystrophy. The Runway of Dreams Foundation, established in 2014, has partnered with Hilfiger Adaptive and Zappos on their adaptive lines, and has grown to become a pioneering organization which promotes empowerment for the disabled community "through fashion and beauty inclusion." Accessibility to fashion is key to the foundation's mission. Through major media campaigns, conferences, university club engagement, and adaptive runway shows, Runway of Dreams has become a major media force in the United States, impacting the way that the fashion and disability story is put into public view.

Other partnerships and collaborations to get adaptive fashions in the public eye have included Faduma's Fellowship partnership with student designer Harriet Eccleston, which represented the first collection at London Fashion Week with wheelchair users as its mainstream target customer. The Spring 2022 collection was shown in September 2021. Harriet partnered with Faduma Farah and the Fellowship Panel, plus Oxford Fashion Studio who represent niche luxury fashion brands, according to their website.

Design of course does not always mean immediate generation of commercial products ready for market. Generation of good ideas for the disabled consumer must include time for discussion with the community, reflection and consideration of what will work best. Many of the designers and advocates that have been mentioned in this book have disability as an aspect of their own lives—either themselves or a family member or friend. This personal link to living as disabled rather than abled provides context, empathy, and creativity in problem-solving. Companies that continually involve the disabled consumer as consultants, creative generators of product ideas and experienced evaluators can truly call themselves inclusive.

No products exist without the generation of a successful idea and The Open Style Lab (OSL) in New York City, founded in 2014 by Grace Jun as a non-profit organization, brings diverse teams of designers, engineers and therapists together with disabled collaborators to brainstorm ideas around different themes. One such example was the Accessible Toolkit, developed at the OSL 2019 Summer program. This toolkit, which was sustainable, accessible and inclusive, contained adaptive sewing tools "to make fashion accessible to people of all abilities." Grace's story can be found in more detail in the next section of this chapter. Open Style Lab, along with other collaborative organizations involving interdisciplinary and community work can be seen as a continuation of the tradition begun by Rusk and Cookman and maintained by *Design without Limits* in the 1980s, demonstrating that the interdisciplinary approach is a successful way of bringing good concepts to market as well as ensuring accessibility, availability, and affordability.

6.3 Design Interviews

Alexandra Palmer on Izzy Camelleri of IZAdaptive

The Canadian designer Izzy Camelleri, founder of IZAdaptive has been groundbreaking in her approach to the field of adaptive fashion. I interviewed Alexandra Palmer, Senior Curator of Fashion at the Royal Ontario Museum, about Izzy Camelleri's work. The exhibition "Fashion Follows Form: Designs for Sitting" at the Royal Ontario Museum in 2014 was one of the first to focus on fashion for disabled consumers, and included designs by Izzy whose line IZAdaptive was "a revolutionary line of fashionable and functional clothing for the growing demographic of men and women who use wheelchairs."[13] Alexandra explained that she first found out about Izzy's work by accident when she walked into the designer's shop in Toronto, curious about the interesting window display. "*She took me into the back and started showing me patterns, and particularly these men's trousers that were cut in a way that eighteenth-century breeches are cut . . . I thought, she's going back to the eighteenth century.*" Alexandra likens this to a lightbulb moment in her own experience as a curator, having never before considered these types of user needs or the research and development involved in figuring out how to make clothing work for disabled bodies. "*The fact that you're sitting in a wheelchair, and you don't have feeling in your lower body and you can't tell if you're sitting on a lumpy seam, or a pocket or anything, and you can die, you can literally die from having bed sores; all of this was nothing that I'd ever been taught or thought about.*"

Alexandra's appreciation and centering of Izzy's work in the exhibition speaks to her respect of the designer's vision: "*The cuts were completely genius. You have to understand about cut; you have to understand how clothes are made to appreciate them.*" Alexandra explained about Izzy's disabled customers having something in common: "*They're sitting so it's an L-shape not an I-shape. That was my light bulb going off and then thinking about how that affects design; because fashion is made for standing people not seated people.*"

Lucy Jones of FFORA

Lucy Jones is CEO of FFORA, an accessories brand directed to wheelchair users. I asked her how she got started designing for disability: "*After a conversation with a younger family member, it was brought to my attention that there really wasn't very much insight and inclusion of people who have disabilities. Since then I've not been able to design any differently other than involve people with disabilities in the design process.*" Lucy rejects the term Adaptive for the type of design that she is doing: "*It begs the question—is this something that we should be ashamed of or something we feel we have to modify? And then I would argue, if we're adapting it, that means it wasn't right for that person from the beginning, so why don't we just make it right from the beginning? . . . The first thing that I did was listen to my family member's experience with clothes, and I wanted to understand how difficult clothes were, so I strapped my arm down and put a sock over my hand. . . . Moving forward though . . . I could always remove the sock and sling at the end of the day, so then I conducted focus groups . . . And of course what I realized was that everyone had a different way of using clothes and a different need. That way of thinking, of making sure that you have a diverse body of people who are testing products is my goal.*"

FFORA's products are luxury wheelchair accessories. Lucy goes on to explain: "*Someone said once in a focus group 'Well, you can't spell accessories without access,' which I loved! The goal was to make sure that the products would find other uses . . . We are constantly surprised when someone has painted over our product, just to show that it's theirs, making it even more personal than before, and I think this shows that this is a community of people who are extremely creative on a day to day basis.*" Lucy's advice to someone wanting to become a designer: "*I would say don't think you know about someone's lifestyle. Go into something with your mind and eyes wide open. Ask the right questions. I think there's room for challenging why we do things the way we do.*" Examples of FFORA's products are shown in Fig. 6.5.

Figure 6.5 *Lucy Jones' FFORA brand—The Everything FFORA Set. Image shows a variety of accessories in black, from the FFORA line. Photo Credit: FFORA*

Grace Jun of OpenStyleLab

Another pioneering contemporary designer working in this space is Grace Jun, CEO of Open Style Lab in New York City, a non-profit that merges design and technology inclusive of people with disabilities. When asked why she was drawn to the area of disability and fashion, she responds; *"That's actually a complex question for me, because in the last few years we saw some attitudes change around products and disabilities, with advertisements in fashion, whether it's Tommy or Zappos. But this change is more personal. About ten years ago, I had an accident that left me with an injury that had me questioning physical challenges related to the body and clothing. So I was considering what design meant in my practice and what I could do when I couldn't use my dominant arm. I remember being unable to get dressed for even a job interview and consequently missing that interview. The experience made me really appreciate the power of independent dressing and the barriers posed by the lack of accessible clothing. And that moment made me a little bit more bold to think outside of the box and I began to think, around package design, why don't we package our body in different ways? That I think became an opportunity to investigate the transformative powers of fashion, which is what I really love, and how people face disempowering circumstances."*

We talked about empathy in the design process and Grace stated: "*I try to stay away from the word empathy because you tend to be absorbed in the other person's emotions, their roller coaster ride of getting through this. But I think it's more. If you love the idea of transformation, whether it's all the shows, the bodies, from Alexander McQeen, or some of the more avant-garde houses, there's a little bit of that, breaking the taboo/mold type of attitude which I feel is innate in fashion and that is exactly the type of energy that I feel when I see people really shine and become the innovative beacon. If I could be so bold I really feel that people with a disability probably are the most innovative because they've had to design within their means, they've had to invent and create things, you know whether they have acquired a disability by birth or by injury . . . No-one's going to think about disability and fashion together.*"

When asked how she sees her body of work fitting in with the kind of movements started by Helen Cookman, Grace responded: "*I think my body of work probably fits in with too many movements! Anywhere from Universal Design to the functional clothing that we've seen historically. It's a question of how this new type of combination of interdisciplinary collaboration is going to be able to dig deep into looking at accessible clothing but also be broad enough to know that you need a lens in functional fabrics or engineering. You need a lens in therapy to be able to think about adaptive clothing, and not just a fashion background. I am trying to figure out myself why the health space has been largely silo-ed and needs a fashion intervention! I think these opportunities go closer and closer until maybe there will be a bunch of fashion designers on staff in hospitals, given what we're experiencing now. And then ask what do these fashion designers then have to learn and have to be able to experience? If you're a fashion designer and you want to work in the healthcare space but you've never worked with people with a disability before, or those who are injured, how is that jump being made? That is what I see our lab mostly doing. That's kind of the feedback I get. [Our Fellows] take on other jobs or residencies or programs that are not related to their initial study.*"

I asked what keeps her motivated knowing how frustrating it is that things have not moved along very quickly. Grace responded "*I think it is definitely my students. I like watching them explore this new territory. OSL is its own non-profit. My board members, we never did this to make money. We did this because we all either have a disability or we have a story, like a grandparent, or a family member. We find it a way to merge our deeper passions that are about social change. Innovation brings such a great spark for everybody. When you have a creative idea, when we're able to talk to someone. That kind of community is so needed and the more that it grows I think it will keep going. I do see the industry changing. They need to be persuaded with different areas like numbers and storytelling, which is so powerful."* I asked her to explain what sort of numbers will be sufficient for persuasion? *"Well, one out of five people in the United States identifies as having a disability of some sort, and I think I saw on a recent report that Parkinson's will really escalate, it was just insane that you're going to ignore this market because you just don't know how to address them."* As for the future of Open Style Lab: *"I hope OSL becomes—more a movement than a company. Hopefully a platform to raise awareness of the cool stuff that's happening, whether it's in different schools or neighborhoods. We have a community to recommend each other's work and then I think it really builds a body of things. It's not just one person doing research. What I'd love to do is build it more robustly with more research from other people that have already shaped or are still shaping the conversation."*

Justin LeBlanc on Justin LeBlanc Design

I interviewed Justin LeBlanc, an independent fashion designer working under the company name Justin LeBlanc Design and a former colleague at NC State University. Justin also teaches fashion design at the higher education level, and was a finalist on Season Twelve of Project Runway, the American reality TV show that focuses on fashion design challenges. As a deaf person, he is a fashion designer with a disability. When asked how he approaches his design process and whether his disability affects this, he states: *"I think being deaf increases my awareness for other disabilities, because I know what it's like to have something where the general public views you differently. I don't view myself as disabled. It's really how society views people and puts them in those specific boxes. I make sure it's all inclusive and what I mean by that term is including all body types. Anyone who might be interested in wearing my clothing and accessories has the opportunity to wear them. It's really just about giving the opportunity to express themselves in fashion no matter what kind of disability, age, size, etc."*

I asked Justin about his teaching approach and how he brings his design practice to the classroom. *"On the academic side of teaching, one of the things I notice is that fashion academic education is broken and the reason I say that is that we focus so much on the models, the fashion show, etc., when we train our students. Even the basic training, what kind of dress form or mannequin we use, they tend to be all size 4–6 [US]. The teacher trains the student to make clothing for these kinds of people. The reality is that does not apply to everyone, so I definitely think you have to go further back into education. Where it begins and where the problem needs to be solved."* When asked to describe his training, given the lack of fashion courses in accessible design, he states: *"So I do have training in fashion design, but when you talk about inclusive or accessible design I don't have training, that's something I had to learn on my own because when I was a student it was not considered important. Now, today, there's a growing need and that is incredible, and I do feel the responsibility to not only continue to educate myself about accessible design or inclusive wear but also to teach my students because that's something I wish I had as a student. Plant the seed and really allow them to think about what inclusive design is. Do we find it in the fashion books, the magazines that we read? Not really, we need to have more exposure to accessible design. So those kids who say they love to look through fashion magazines when they were a child and grow up to be fashion designers, we need to start implementing more accessible design so the younger generation see that and they can aspire to be an accessible designer."*

Regarding his current inclusive design philosophy: *"I've been in the business for seven years and since the very beginning I've been more focused on expressing through fashion to educate people about deaf culture. It's not so much adaptive, It's more about changing their perspective into seeing what I see. My garments are all very textural. It falls back on me being a visual person since I'm deaf and always looking at texture—it speaks to me in a way. I would hope that accessible wear design can be normalized. When I say that, I mean that people who have a disability and people who don't will buy the same product. I've never seen that at retail. If I go into a retail store to find that clothing, most likely it's not there. It's something that has to be ordered online."*

Justin's marketing approach is in line with most other fashion businesses: "*My current marketing is primarily through social media, Instagram has been the main social media platform because it's a visual marketing tool, and Instagram is very savvy in supporting small businesses. This is definitely the main source of marketing, alongside events relating to niche people, like the deaf community. I socialize and network with these people. So it tends to be social media and word of mouth and I have a website for people to look at.*" He would tell someone who's interested in becoming a designer: "*Meet the people they're designing for. They can learn from their teachers and books, they can design prototypes but nothing is more important than meeting the people they're designing for. They will provide such important information.*"

These four interviews reveal some common threads. The designers have either experienced disability personally or through family members. They feel that the fashion industry and fashion education need to change. Regarding their advice to aspiring designers, they also give the following pieces of advice: (1) Meet the people you are designing for; (2) Experience the lifestyle however you can; (3) Become interdisciplinary; and (4) Learn from the creative experiences of the people who have been living with adaptation and creativity all their lives.

6.4 Do we have a Disability Design Process?

In the book *Design Justice,* Costanza-Chock argues for a change in the way we design products:

> . . . an adaptive design that enables personalization and flexible configuration of shared core objects, tools, platforms and systems . . . A paradigm shift to design that is meant to actively dismantle, rather than unintentionally reinforce, the matrix of domination, requires that we retool. This means that there is a need to develop intersectional user stories, testing approaches, training data, benchmarks, standards, validation processes, and impact assessments, among many other tools.
>
> COSTANZA-CHOCK, 2020: 54[14]

In higher education, fashion pedagogical practice tends to be rooted either in the aesthetic (art-based) or functional (engineering-based) educational models, with the former being the traditional paradigm, and with many institutions blending both models. The functional field has been slower to integrate into curricula, undoubtedly since if offers a less "sexy" side of fashion with fewer external visual marketing opportunities to entice potential students and give a wow factor to the general public. In addition, from a teaching and learning perspective, the functional/engineering approach has received less coverage by the academic press, resulting in fewer textbooks that address and integrate the more "functional" aspects of fashion design, akin to what Justin LeBlanc mentioned in his interview. Many instructors and students working in this field are familiar with the first comprehensive textbook to focus on the design and development of functional clothing design, which was Susan Watkins' *Clothing: The Portable Environment*, first published in 1984 and republished in 1995.[15] The text was aimed at university students in clothing design programs to give them an overview of the functional, occupational and physiological needs of clothing users for "specialist" situations, but disability was not included. A new edition, published in 2015 with co-author Lucy Dunne, moves towards an incorporation of disability by including a chapter on "Designing Clothing for people with medical conditions and Physical Handicaps," under the heading "Designs for Special Populations."[16] However, the section is more of a guide to how students can find specific information on body and clothing systems elsewhere in the book, acknowledging "Although designers would probably prefer to have precise formulas to solve problems for each user population, the specific needs ... are so varied that it would take many volumes to do this." (Watkins and Dunne 2015: 348)

Many current designers trained through the US educational system are perhaps familiar with Jane Lamb and Mary Jo Kallal's "Functional, Expressive and Aesthetic (FEA) Consumer Needs Model," which advocates a three-pronged approach, ensuring that the customer's physical and psychological needs are met in any response to a design project brief.[17] This article has over 550 citations according to Google Scholar as of June 2022 (the average citation of academic articles is less than ten). The FEA model, with a publication date just after passage of the ADA in 1990, acknowledges and advocates for the need for aesthetics and self-expression in fashion design for disabled people. Lamb and Kallal present a design framework that is holistic, folding function, aesthetics and self-expression into a blended system. They acknowledge the lack of aesthetic qualities of most of the work on clothing for disabled people in the 1980s. Their rationale ties in well with the passage of ADA and indeed many of the opinions in this chapter; "Thinking of design for special needs as just another part of a general design framework is a natural parallel to the way people with special needs want to be considered" (Lamb and Kallal 1992: 42).[18] Lamb and Kallal's work is significant in that it incorporates a formalized approach to user needs found in Systems Engineering, as well as acknowledging the role that cultural influences play on consumer choice, using the terms "customary use" and "standards of beauty," (Lamb and Kallal 1992: 43) which brings design for disabled people in line with a formalized process already in use with traditional fashion design thinking. Lamb and Kallal's work on the FEA model was followed by a host of other researchers in the 1990s and beyond, who used the model to document the adaptation of a design process to include disability and embrace aesthetic and expressive needs in the process: "Rather than assuming that a client or target market wants function *or* expression *or* beauty, designers using the present framework assume that intended wearers want function *and* expression *and* beauty." (Lamb and Kallal 1992: 46).

Whatever process is being utilized, designers understand that there is a flow to conceiving an idea and planning its execution. Multiple elements are utilized from start to finish depending on the context and the desired outcome. Designers have a toolbox consisting of elements (color, line, texture, shape, and form) and principles (unity, movement, repetition, focus, contrast, and balance) to help guide the process. In the fashion design world, are these same tools being used to figure out how to design for disabled bodies beyond the functional and engineering demands of a project?

Over the past few decades of work into design for the disabled consumer, research outcomes have shown how to technically manipulate a pattern or engineer a material so that garments can fit, stretch, wrap, and fasten around bodies with the least amount of stressors to the wearer and the most comfort. But have the aesthetic tools of design been effectively harnessed in equal proportions? Multiple guidelines already define existing fashion and beauty systems based on skin tone, eye/hair color and body shape in order to determine fabrication, details, and silhouette so that aesthetic impact for a target customer or groups is maximized. Personal color analysts and wardrobe stylists abound to help people present their best external self, but are these stylists and guidelines equally accessible to the disabled fashion customer? We have seen exploration of such systems advocated to improve design in Quinn and Chase's book *Design without Limits*, which was discussed in the previous chapter. Chapter Two of Quinn and Chase's book reminds us that the tools of fashion, including Line, Shape, Color, Texture, Pattern and Proportion, can be harnessed to achieve outcomes that address user's aesthetic, expressive and functional needs.

We have witnessed over the centuries, in the absence of available and satisfactory products in the marketplace, disabled consumers designing, adapting and innovating to develop the products that they, their families and their friends need. This is not a phenomenon exclusive to the disabled community. Eric Von Hippel shows that certain groups of users with unmet needs will develop and share innovative products with others, because industries do not consider their needs to merit production or benefit from economies of scale.[19] Users with lived experience in the design challenge must therefore be more intentionally incorporated into the process in order to blend the adaptation and innovation of lived experience with the abilities of industry to produce and disseminate suitable products on a global scale. In any design process, co-design and participatory design could be the keys to solving problems now that we live in an industrialized society where corporations are who we look to for products and services.

One of the methods typically used to gain empathetic vision about a design problem that is now being challenged is disability simulation, where abled designers "put themselves into the shoes of" someone with a particular disability in order to gain insight into user experience:

Abled designers typically focus on an ableist approach to technically modifying or augmenting the individual bodies of Disabled people to approximate normative mobility styles, compared to Disabled people, who may be more interested in architectural and infrastructural changes that fit their own mobility needs.

COSTANZA-CHOCK, 2020: 84[20]

No matter how the process itself is being designed, what is being advocated on all levels is further inclusion of diversity of users on a design team throughout the product design process and a fresh approach making use of all the tools we have at our disposal.

6.5 Harnessing Technological Developments

At the same time that I am writing this book, technology is transforming fashion on multiple levels on an almost daily basis. Data-mining tools are ramping up ways to segment customers into demographic units and micro-define user needs. Bodies are being scanned to determine accurate measurements, from which refined avatars are being created so that a 3D digital body double can be used to design, fit, and simulate a garment on a person before a physical fit model is needed for verification, thereby avoiding the need for multiple prototypes and physical fit sessions. 3D printing and robotics are transforming the manufacturing process and enabling production of items on an as-needed basis. Auxetic, phase-change and other smart fabrics are tapping into the mechanics and biorhythms of the human body to manage and regulate health and performance. Magnetic, sonic and laser technology are inviting new ways of joining materials together. If one believes that technology can inform and assist the creative process, then these available technologies, some of which are now available at the consumer level, must be utilized to rethink how to make our fashion inclusive and accessible.

Materials development is an aspect of technology that has vast potential to assist in inclusively designed fashion. Two friends who went from hacking code to "hacking clothes, making more comfortable dress shirts and socks from their favorite athletic gear" founded Ministry of Supply clothing company at Massachusetts Institute of Technology (MIT) in Cambridge, Massachusetts.[21] The company uses Phase Change technology developed by NASA to thermo-regulate body temperature, and add wicking, odor and bacterial control to materials for its dress shirts. The company is motivated, focused and has diversified into many collaborations, but has kept comfort as a core value. With this in mind, they are now producing the Kinetic Adaptive Pant for Women and Men, in navy and black. The website states that the pants were developed in collaboration with the Stavros Center for Independent Living and the collaboration of Gold-Medalist US Paralympians. The main material in the pants is the Kinetic line of fabric, a warp knit with four-way stretch, moisture-wicking properties and water repellency, which is made from 100 percent polyester fiber (15 percent corn-based).

Another area of materials development which holds promise is 3D printing. UNYQ (pronounced: unique) is a startup that sells 3D-printed prosthetic leg covers. The company calls themselves "the leaders in digitalized prosthetic wears."[22] The company's co-founder, Eythor Bender, recognized how difficult it is to make new technology accessible to the people who need it, so prices were cut in half, sourcing was improved and scaled up. The company is transparent about its process and available on a global scale, with clinic providers on every continent. They also own their production facilities and have a vibrant online community, known as UNYQers.

Summary

Interest in the design of fashionable products for disabled consumers has seen a marked increase in the last decade, due to both social and technological reasons. What is most perplexing is the lack of "trickle-down" to an affordable retail level. While some products have been made available at retail at affordable prices, accessibility is still lagging behind innovation.

I have by no means presented a comprehensive survey of everything that has been happening at the intersection of disability and fashion design since 2010, but hopefully there is some interesting information here to consider, and my main takeaways based on this information are as follows:

- We should look to the history of all cultures for design inspiration and ideas. We have already established that for centuries, garments have been adapted to change the shape of the body in intricate ways and to engineer easier access. We know that Queen Alexandra's dressmakers used ingenious pattern and embellishment engineering to create an appearance of symmetry. Using historic examples can help us look at design work a bit differently and re-examine some of our processes

- As expressed by Grace Jun, designers should become familiar with the healthcare system so that the fields can be more blended and interchangeable. Academic research leadership must continue to move the field forward, disseminate knowledge and promote global discussion. The Textile Institute recently issued a journal, consisting of a number of case studies about the design of "specialty" garments: a stoma bag; a urine bag; pants for people who are wheelchair users; and sun block protective garments.[23] The section on future prospects suggests the following ideas for research:

  - Using sensors in clothing for detection of problems
  - Developing eco-friendly and reusable items
  - Developing electronic assistive devices such as exo-skeletons and robotic clothing to help people move parts of their body
  - Microencapsulation—grafting medication onto textile fibers to aid in medicine delivery

- Annotated bibliographies and literature reviews must continue to be published on the topic. In 2002 a comprehensive review on the topics of clothing and disability was published by Dr Usha Chowdhary, with research articles organized into fifty categories, covering research produced in the US up to that point, including extension publications; magazine articles; catalogs; government support and community resources.[24] This is one important way in which new knowledge can be passed along and new designers venturing into the field can broaden their education.

- Organizations and R&D facilities must continue to drive change, innovation and above all, promote product inclusivity. In Japan, the non-profit organization UNIFA, was established in 2001 with a mission as follows: "By promoting 'universal fashion,' which aims to create a society where everyone can enjoy rich fashion regardless of age, body shape, disability, gender, nationality, etc., we will contribute to the promotion of profits for the general public"[25]

- Suitable training and exposure to end users is key so that students understand the "normalizing" of disabled customers within the mainstream fashion industry. Clearly there is a benefit to having a set of guidelines and models (such as the FEA model and Watkins' work) for designers-in-training and those new to the task of designing for disability. However, years of applied study of body systems, pattern manipulation, and materials innovation have not produced a system whereby fashion offerings for disabled consumers at the retail level have improved. If all trainee fashion designers are taught to integrate inclusivity into product lines, the industry cannot help but change from within. Having supportive designers and developers on company staff who do not treat disabled people as a "specialized" market can parallel the "pull" for products that is coming from the current consumer movement for inclusivity.

In addition, as an endnote to this contemporary chapter, there is a new line of Barbie dolls with disabilities. I'm super curious about how the fashions will be designed . . .

Notes

1   ADA.gov (n.d.), Introduction to the Americans with Disabilities Act. Available online: https://www.ada.gov/ada_intro.htm (accessed November 1, 2022).

2   US Dept. of Justice Civil Rights Division (2022), ADA Standards for Accessible Design Title III Regulation 28 CRF Part 36 (1991). Available online: https://www.ada.gov/law-and-regs/design-standards/1991-design-standards/ (accessed December 27, 2022).

3   Ibid.

4   Legislation.gov.uk (2022), *Disability Discrimination Act 1995 Part III Discrimination in other areas: Goods, facilities and services.* Available online: https://www.legislation.gov.uk/ukpga/1995/50/part/III (accessed December 27, 2022).

5   United Nations (2022), *10ᵗʰ anniversary of the adoption of Convention on the Rights of Persons with Disabilities (CRPD)*. Available online: https://www.un.org/development/desa/disabilities/convention-on-the-rights-of-persons-with-disabilities/the-10th-anniversary-of-the-adoption-of-convention-on-the-rights-of-persons-with-disabilities-crpd-crpd-10.html (accessed December 27, 2022).

6   European Commission (2021), *United Nations Convention on the Rights of Persons with Disabilities*. Available online: https://ec.europa.eu/social/main.jsp?catId=1138&langId=en (accessed December 27, 2022).

7   Campbell, R. (1747), *The London Tradesman*, originally published by T. Gardner, London in 1747. Reprinted by Augustus M. Kelley, Publishers, New York, 1969.

8   Target (2023), *Future at Heart: Cat and Jack Adaptive*. Available online: https://corporate.target.com/press/multimedia?selectedTab=assets&query=Cat%20%26%20Jack%20adaptive&page=1&sortOrder=desc (accessed January 9, 2023).

9   Ibid.

10   Target (2022), *Cat & Jack™*. Available online: https://www.target.com/p/toddler-girls-adaptive-abdominal-access-tie-dye-jumpsuit-cat-jack-blue/-/A-84082600 (accessed May 20, 2022).

11   Ravenscroft, T. (2021), *Nike reveals hands-free GO FlyEase trainer*, Dezeen, Feb 1, 2021. Available online: https://www.dezeen.com/2021/02/01/nike-go-flyease-trainer-hands-free/ (accessed October 27, 2022).

12   The Active Amputee (2017), *Amazing Prosthetic Covers by ALLELLES*, August 23, 2017. Available online: https://www.theactiveamputee.org/2017/08/23/amazing-prosthetic-covers-by-alleles/ (accessed October 27, 2022).

13   ROM (2014), Fashion Follows Form: Designs for Sitting. Available online: https://www.rom.on.ca/en/exhibitions-galleries/exhibitions/fashion-follows-form-designs-for-sitting (accessed October 27, 2022).

14   Costanza-Chock, S. (2020), *Design Justice: Community-led Practices to Build the Worlds we Need,* Cambridge, MA: The M.I.T. Press.

15   Watkins, S.M. (1984), *Clothing: The Portable Environment*, (revised 1995), Ames, IA: Iowa State University Press.

16   Watkins, S.M. and Dunne, L. (2015), *Functional Clothing Design: From Sportswear to Spacesuits*, New York: Fairchild Books.

17   Lamb, J.M. and Kallal, M.J. (1992), "A Conceptual Framework for Apparel Design", *Clothing and Textiles Research Journal*, 10 (2): 42–7.

18   Ibid.

19   Von Hippel, E. (2005), *Democratizing Innovation*, Cambridge, MIT Press.

20   Costanza-Chock, S. (2020), *Design Justice: Community-led Practices to Build the Worlds we Need*, Cambridge, MA: The M.I.T. Press.

21 Ministry of Supply, (2022), *A Decade of Innovation in Comfort*. Available online: https://www.ministryofsupply.com/about/innovation-in-comfort (accessed October 27, 2022).

22 UNYQ, (2022), *Design Innovation*. Available online: https://unyq.com/about-unyq/ (accessed October 27, 2022).

23 Textile Institute, (2011), "Development of medical garments and apparel for the elderly and the disabled", *Textile Progress*, 43 (4).

24 Chowdhary, U. (2002), "Aesthetics and function in clothing for people with special needs". *Proceedings: EASYTEX 2002, 1st International Conference on Clothing and Textiles for Disabled and Elderly People*, Tampere, Finland, pp.1–8.

25 UNIFA, (2022), *Japan Universal Fashion Association*. Available online: https://www.unifa.jp/ (accessed October 27, 2022).

7

A Story of Disabled Makers

Introduction

Much of this book has been devoted to wearers, users and aficionados of fashion, but disabled people have also participated in fashion as creators and makers of products that connect with the fashion market, from mass-production to single item art pieces. In many cases, the interaction of disabled people with the creation of fashion-related products—both commercial and art-based—have been examples of social entrepreneurship activities, to which the first section of this chapter is almost exclusively devoted. However, there are also situations of necessity driving creative activity and more recently, the need for self-expression and self-actualization as disabled designers are able to function within industry parameters, thanks to greater acceptance and awareness. This chapter will highlight a selection of stories about disabled people who have interacted with fashion on a variety of artistic and creative levels, first in a historical context, and then on the contemporary scene to examine how opportunities are presenting themselves in the modern world.

7.1 Disabled Makers in History

Throughout history, evidence shows that disabled people have been creatively involved with innovation and adaptation of clothing for their end use. The first example of creating selected for this chapter is not directly fashion-related, but clothing played an important and creative part in the life of this artist. Sarah Biffin (1784–50) was born with phocomelia, meaning that she had no arms and legs, and grew to be thirty-seven inches tall as an adult. She was "exhibited" as a fairground attraction in England, and known alternatively as The Limbless Wonder and the Eighth Wonder. In order to develop skills, Sarah taught herself how to sew and paint with her mouth and became a well-respected artist (her customers included Queen Victoria). In her self-portraits, Sarah represents herself with a paintbrush sewn into the sleeve of her cloak, thereby using clothing to demonstrate her choice of profession. Her intentional use of fashionable artistic dress for self-portraiture sent a message that her appearance and artistic profession are inextricably linked. She proudly states that she is an artist, she is disabled and she uses fashion to assist her work. Fig. 7.1 shows this proud attitude, her fashionable dress, and the paintbrush stitched to the border of her artist's cape. To be represented as an artist using the convention of headwear and cloak was common in self-portraiture at this time. Sarah's disability is somewhat minimized in this portrait by the cloak worn over her black gown, but her paintbrush is clearly visible attached to the right shoulder of her cloak.

According to the Philip Mould & Co. website, another self-portrait showing her paintbrush stitched directly to the shoulder of her gown, and painted at the height of her fame in the early 1820s, is her best known work. The painting sold at auction in December 2021 for £137,000, despite Sotheby's 2019 estimates being closer to £1,200–£1,800. Much could be made of the monetary significance of the portrait (a miniature) but it validates her reputation as an independent and enterprising woman with a studio in Bond Street, London, obtaining a steady income from her art in the early nineteenth century. The fact that she sets herself up in artistic dress in the tradition of painters such as Rembrandt is testament to her confidence in her abilities and work. Above all, her fashionable clothing has been adapted to facilitate her work and act as an extension of the tools she used to execute her art.

Other famous figures of the nineteenth century, already discussed in earlier chapters, had agency in their clothing design and construction. Lord Nelson sketched designs and ideas for the visor attached to the front of his hat, and

Figure 7.1 *Miss Biffin. Painted by herself without hands, 1842, signed and dated. Watercolor and gouache on card. Sarah shows herself here in "artistic" and fashionable dress of the times with her paintbrush stitched to her cloak. Image courtesy of Philip Mould & Co.*

Lavinia Warren sewed using an adapted sewing machine prior to her wardrobe being created by the designers of the day. It is unknown if Lavinia had any input into the gowns that Barnum commissioned from the Houses of Worth and Demorest. It is also unknown whether Lord Raglan was involved in the design and development of the sleeve to which he lends his name. Research uncovered very little about the design origins of the sleeve and its subsequent integration into a bespoke military coat, despite investigation into both his life and the archives of Aquascutum.

In the twentieth century, I have chosen to report two stories from the United Kingdom that were born out of volunteer efforts to support disabled soldiers returning from active duty in the First World War. The first story is that of the Disabled Soldiers' Embroidery Industry, established in 1918 by Ernest Thesiger. The idea behind the organization was to use embroidery as a therapeutic tool to treat survivors of combat trauma sustained in the trenches of mainland Europe. The veterans were taught to embroider during home visits or via instructions that were mailed to them, and all the pieces were designed so that they could be made in their homes, thereby enabling the veterans to remain in a place that was convenient for them.

Records stated that the overall health of the veteran workers improved after being enrolled in the program—men reported that sewing was "good for the nerves" and that it thwarted "melancholy." Compensation for the piecework was substantial: a man could earn the equivalent of half his weekly veteran's pension making embroidery. The pieces were worked mostly in gros-point and petit-point, and primarily resulted in church and home furnishings, however there were commercial business agreements set up with Pearsall's threads and Weldon's pattern-makers.

Joseph McBrinn explains how "The mainstay of the organization's sales throughout the 1920s and 1930s was small items aimed at middle-class female consumers, including reproductions of historic tapestries, needlework pictures, bedcovers, children's clothes, furniture covers, personal items such as purses and handbags and miscellaneous household goods from waste paper baskets and garden aprons to playing-card cases."[1] (McBrinn 2015: 24) After the death of the founder Ernest Thesiger, the company shut down in 1955. The pieces shown in Figs 7.2 to 7.4 show views of some of the fashion accessories in the collection of the Bucks Museum in Aylesbury, England, home of the national collection of the Embroiderers' Guild.

McBrinn explains how the organization "affords some insight into how masculine identity and the disabled body have operated as active rather than passive agents in design history."[2] (McBrinn 2016: 1) The Disabled Soldiers' Embroidery Industry was not the only therapeutically-driven enterprise to come out of the First World War, but its process, output and marketing, along with the founder's personality and enthusiasm, make it a model for therapy

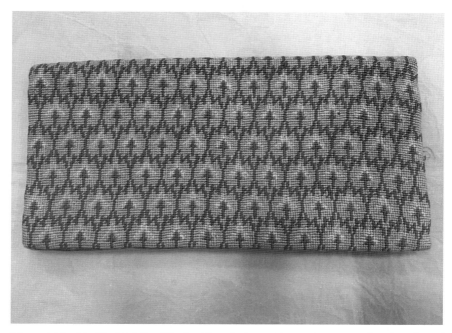

Figure 7.2 *Disabled Soldiers' Embroidery Industry Purse. Courtesy of Embroiderers' Guild National Collection, Bucks Museum, Aylesbury, Buckinghamshire, England*

Figure 7.3 *Label for "Soldiers Embroidery Industry," stitched inside purse shown in Figure 7.2. Courtesy of Embroiderers' Guild National Collection, Bucks Museum, Aylesbury, Buckinghamshire, England*

and intervention which meets the patient at their own level and gives them a sense of accomplishment through beautiful handworked needlecraft.

The second story, that of Annie Bindon Carter (see Fig. 7.5) and Painted Fabrics, Inc., a company based in Sheffield, England and operational for almost fifty years, is another story of an initiative that started out as a volunteer effort

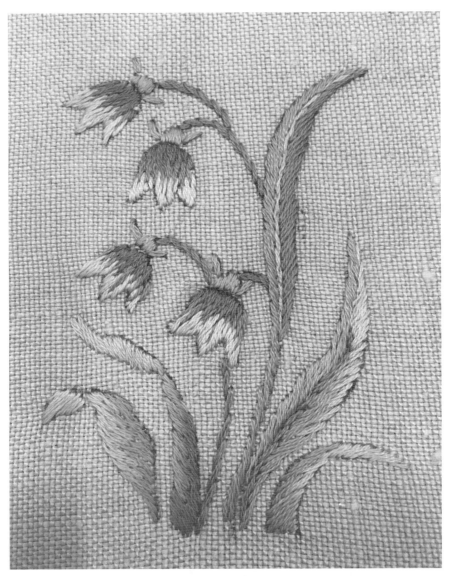

Figure 7.4 *Detail of embroidered flower on a panel piece in the Embroiderers' Guild collection. Courtesy of Embroiderers' Guild National Collection, Bucks Museum, Aylesbury, Buckinghamshire, England*

involving disabled veterans from the First World War in the creation of fashion fabrics and products. By the mid-1920s, the company which grew out of the original therapeutic effort was supplying products to the most wealthy and fashionable people in the United Kingdom.

Figure 7.5 *Annie Bindon Carter, founder of Painted Fabrics, Inc., Sheffield, England. Photo Credit: Sheffield City Archives: PF/4/2/3/1/18*

Annie Bindon Carter, a graduate of the Sheffield School of Art, volunteered at Wharncliffe War Hospital in Sheffield as a student during the First World War. Many of the veterans for whom she was volunteering had lost limbs, and in trying to teach patients at the facility to stencil as a hobby, she realized that if she attached a brush to an arm stump, a veteran could apply paint through the stencil and onto fabric secured underneath, thereby creating a stenciled fabric piece. The idea grew in popularity and support, and in 1923 Annie leased a disused Army camp at Norton Woodseats in Sheffield, turning a former

Army barracks into print and dye houses where the veterans could do their work. This became the Painted Fabrics workshop.

Like Thesiger's workers, Annie's crew were well compensated. They were paid one shilling per hour and were guaranteed thirty hours a week's work. As the fabric lines expanded into sewn products, the men also did some of the stitching, using adapted sewing machines, which allowed "everything from picot edging to hem stitching" (McBrinn 2019: 296).[3] The operation was a model for community living, combining the textile industry studios with adapted accommodation for the workers and their families, as well as small-scale farming facilities.

The designs for the fabrics were created by Annie, along with Dorothy Carter (her sister), Phyllis Lawton and Edith Jagger (all of whom studied at Sheffield School of Art) and some of their original stencils survive in the Sheffield Archives (see Fig. 7.7). However, a senior archivist explains how "Production ... was firmly the domain of the disabled workers, with talk of modifications to tools of production that were presumably made by

Figure 7.6 *Disabled veterans from the Painted Fabrics Workshop. Photo Credit: Sheffield City Archives: PF/4/2/4*

Figure 7.7 *Original stencil design used in the Painted Fabrics Workshop. Photo Credit: Sheffield City Archives: PF/4/5/2*

both ABC [Annie Bindon Carter] and the workers to suit each person's individual needs."[4]

The company motto was "Work Not Charity." Annie claimed that Painted Fabrics employed "a larger percentage of very seriously disabled than any other ex-service men's establishments ..."[5] Princess Mary (the Princess Royal and the late Queen Elizabeth II's aunt) officially opened the "campus" in 1925, and was the company's Royal Patron, even getting involved by selling pieces at some of the sales. With Royal support and unique adaptive workspaces, Painted Fabrics was a very successful example among the many charitable organizations set up after the First World War with a goal of helping disabled veterans back into employment.

Painted Fabrics' business model was unique. Products were sold at exhibitions and hotels in exclusive invitation-only sales, as well as in wealthy private citizens' homes. Yardage of fabric was also available through Liberty of London, although unfortunately no fabric samples exist in their archive. At the 1937 annual exhibition at Claridge's of London (a luxury 5-star hotel), Her Majesty Queen Elizabeth the Queen Mother attended and bought two dresses for the Princesses

Figure 7.8 *Plaque on exterior wall of Sheffield City Housing Development, where the new brick building still bears the name Painted Fabrics. Photo Credit: Author, 2021*

Elizabeth and Margaret. Demand was so high for the sale that Scotland Yard (the London police establishment) were brought in to control the traffic. The breadth of Painted Fabric's product offerings is explained as follows:

> The former Army huts produced luxurious clothing and hand-crafted pieces, from cushion covers to specially commissioned wedding dresses. Commercially they produced altar frontals and a variety of furnishings for private houses, including curtains for Princess Mary's boudoir on her wedding day.[6]

McBrinn (2016) explains how Countess Maud Fitzwilliam, "a fashionable hostess of Edwardian and interwar society" was both a friend of Annie Carter and a loyal customer, purchasing curtains, a bedspread, and her "court train, to which [the] Princess Royal drew the King's attention" (letter from Countess Fitzwilliam to Annie Carter, McBrinn 2016: 291).[7]

The impact of Annie's work with Painted Fabrics is not widely recognized in mainstream fashion or textile history. However, the social impact of Painted Fabrics was recognized when she was awarded the Member of the Most Excellent Order of the British Empire (MBE) in 1926 for the positive impact of her transformative therapeutic work with disabled veterans. In terms of artistic merit of the work produced by the company, Annie Carter wrote:

> The designs as suggested by me and adapted from many sources are of necessity grown by force of circumstances mainly due to disability . . . Dr Rothenstein the director of the Tate Gallery always stresses this point . . . his point in every case has been that Painted Fabrics was developing a new and interesting English Peasant Industry and that the patterning as so evolved was of intense historical interest. As in all matters relating to art the question of whether you like the work or not is debatable and personal. I may here say that Dr Rothenstein is the only person who has completely understood Painted Fabrics' work.[8]

Annie's writings suggest that the art had strong contemporary artistic value, which seems to have been one of her main goals for the company. Evidence shows that Painted Fabrics' upholstery textiles were also expensive, costing hundreds of pounds at the time, making them only accessible to the extremely wealthy. The company stopped production during the Second World War and was not able to scale back up afterwards, so the final sale was held in 1958, and the company shut down at that point.

The fashionable garments that were designed and made by Painted Fabrics tended to be simple in silhouette, possibly to create plenty of focus on the surface stencil work, but also perhaps to allow the products themselves to be constructed by the veterans. The following photographs represent a selection of pieces in the collection of the City of Sheffield, which have been donated by former owners over a number of years, and which I was fortunate to be allowed access to examine first-hand. Fig. 7.9 shows a pink silk ladies' blouse, dated around 1930. The silhouette of the garment is a simple T-shape, somewhat akin to the simple blouses worn by Frida Kahlo, with a round neck, and elasticized hem, which gathers to the waist of the wearer. The decoration consists of five stenciled geometric flowers in a horizontal placement across the chest of the blouse (see detail in Fig. 7.10). The horizontal decoration continues across the blouse in the form of stylized plant stems and geometric borders around the sleeves.

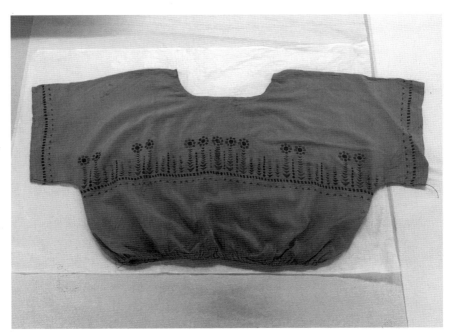

Figure 7.9 *Painted Fabrics pink silk blouse showing horizontal stenciled patterns. Collection of Museums Sheffield, Weston Park Museum, Sheffield, UK. Photo Credit: Author, 2021*

Figure 7.10 *Painted Fabrics pink silk blouse showing detail of horizontal stenciled patterns. Collection of Museums Sheffield, Weston Park Museum, Sheffield, UK. Photo Credit: Author, 2021*

Fig. 7.11 shows another fashionable ladies' garment worn in the early 1930s. This blue velvet cape has a high padded and ornamented collar, and is decorated with stenciled flowers, which flow in colored swags around the garment. The design is not "mirrored" at center front, which may indicate lack of sophistication in working out the design. It may also be representative of the fact that the garment was cut from continuously printed stenciled yardage, which would be the most simple cutting method, rather that realigning each side of the front so that the left and right side are "mirrored"—a process that takes up more time, labor and fabric.

A close-up detail of the stencil work can be seen in Fig. 7.12, clearly showing the cracks in the pigment used for the decoration sitting on top of the velvet fabric.

Inside the cape (Fig. 7.13), one can see the silk lining, which was also stenciled in a similar color to the exterior of the cape, with small geometric and abstract floral patterns. Even though the body of the lining is still in good condition, at the top of the cape, the lining is in less favorable condition around the inside neck, suggesting perhaps that this garment did see some wear by the user, though at the time of writing, no photographs could be found to identify the wearer or the occasion.

Fig. 7.14 shows one of the most unique pieces in the Weston Park collection, which is cataloged as a wedding dress. I chose to show a detail of the print design of this piece because it does not have the typical repeat pattern design of the other garments and accessories in the collection; instead it represents a more "conversational" motif in the form of Asian-inspired architecture.

All Painted Fabrics products that were for sale had their own label attached, and Fig. 7.15 shows a detail of a nightdress with the original label still pinned to it.

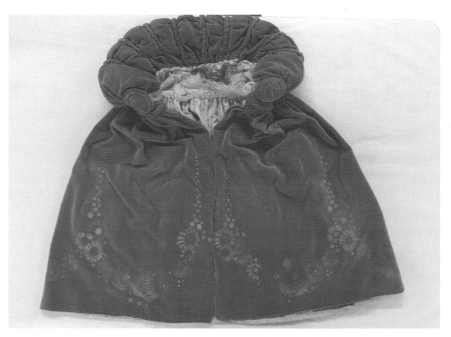

Figure 7.11 *Painted Fabrics ladies' cape. Collection of Museums Sheffield, Weston Park Museum, Sheffield, UK. Photo Credit: Author, 2021*

Figure 7.12 *Detail of stenciling, showing the cracks in pigment, which occurs when color sits "on top of" fabric, rather than forming a chemical dye bond with the fibers. Collection of Museums Sheffield, Weston Park Museum, Sheffield, UK. Photo Credit: Author, 2021*

Weston Park collection also has socks, known as "stump socks," used by the Painted Fabrics workers to put over their amputated limbs while they were working in the studio. These are shown in Fig. 7.16.

As previously mentioned, little is known about the ownership of these items prior to them entering the Weston Park collection. Collecting has been sporadic over the years, and sometimes the pieces have come into the collection without any identification other than the donor's word that these are Painted Fabrics

Figure 7.13 *Cape interior with printed lining and fabric decomposition inside the collar. Collection of Museums Sheffield, Weston Park Museum, Sheffield, UK. Photo Credit: Author, 2021*

products. In the Sheffield Archives, written and print records support the history—both artistic and economic. Fig. 7.17 shows one of the original fashion sketches, which, according to the caption, was designed for the Mayor of Batley (another town in Yorkshire, the county in which Sheffield is located). Marketing images were as sophisticated as a major fashion house, as shown in Fig. 7.18, which depicts a model wearing a Painted Fabrics coat with stenciled pattern.

The stories of the Disabled Soldiers' Embroidery Industry and Painted Fabrics are not necessarily peculiar to the times nor innovative in their objectives. Their uniqueness lies in the creativity and diligence of both Ernest Thesiger and Annie Bindon Carter to create authenticity in their work and the sense of community that was crafted for employees and in the case of Painted Fabrics, their families. Art and craft therapy continues to be incorporated into physical and cognitive rehabilitation programs, though not on the same commercial scale as Painted Fabrics, and there are multiple military therapy

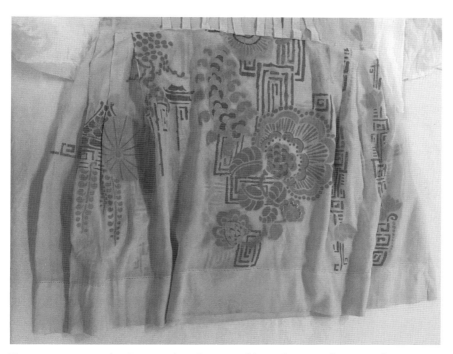

Figure 7.14 *Detail of Painted Fabrics wedding dress. Collection of Museums Sheffield, Weston Park Museum, Sheffield, UK. Photo Credit: Author, 2021*

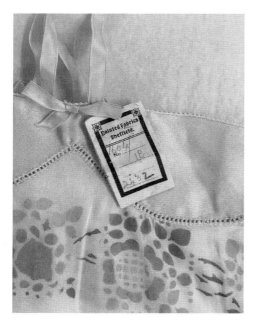

Figure 7.15 *Detail of nightgown showing stencil pattern and PF label. Collection of Museums Sheffield, Weston Park Museum, Sheffield, UK. Photo Credit: Author, 2021*

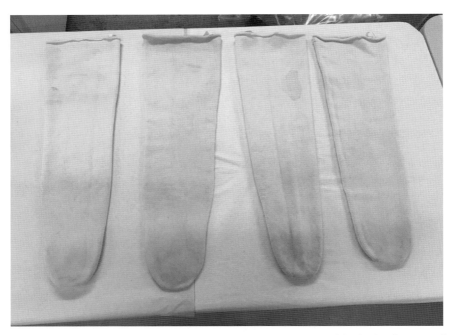

Figure 7.16 *"Stump socks" worn by veterans over amputated limbs. Collection of Museums Sheffield, Weston Park Museum, Sheffield, UK. Photo Credit: Author, 2021*

programs that engage disabled veterans in artistic pursuits. What stands out about Carter and Thesiger is that they addressed the workers' needs at least as much as considering product development and commercialization; Carter by providing adapted workspaces for veterans and creating an entire community around the print works, and Thesiger by taking the work to and from soldiers' houses, akin to a centuries-old business system of "putting-out" work to domestic individual craftspeople. It is worth noting that no new technology or business model was needed for either of these entrepreneurs, just a commitment to enable workers to earn a living wage and the opportunity to contribute using the assets that they had available to them.

Later in the twentieth century, it is worth restating that Helen Cookman of Functional Fashions was deaf and had originally designed a dress that concealed her hearing aids. Similarly, Mrs. Van Davis Odell and Mr. Leinenweber were disabled, and operated successful mainstream clothing businesses for a number of years. These stories and others about designers/business owners are integrated into ch. 4.

Figure 7.17 *Fashion sketch for a Painted Fabrics design for the Mayor of Batley, Yorkshire. City of Sheffield Archives, Sheffield, UK. Photo Credit: Sheffield City Archives: PF/4/5/1*

Figure 7.18 *Publicity photo for a Painted Fabrics garment. City of Sheffield Archives, Sheffield, UK. Photo Credit: Sheffield City Archives: PF/4/2/7, Picture Sheffield ref. arc00633*

7.2 The Legacy of Disabled Makers

What is the impact of these individual stories and commercial enterprises on today's makers and on the changing fashion industry? In many countries, therapy through craft is still widely practiced. One of the pioneers in the United States is Help Heal Veterans, a 501(c)(3) company founded in 1971 which sends free craft kits to hospitalized and homebound disabled veterans.[9] Crafts include woodwork, leatherwork and jewelry, and the kits use recycled materials, committing themselves to sustainability as well as therapy, rehabilitation and recovery. The model of kit delivery to the veterans' homes is straight out of the playbook of Ernest Thesiger. There is no cost for the kits—they are all donor supported—veterans can also receive kits in a medical facility or nursing home. In addition, there are a few craft care centers scattered around the country. The response to the kits is as positive as the First World War veterans who spoke about the way in which practicing embroidery relieved the "melancholy" and "thwarted the nerves." Again from the Help Heal Veterans website: "Doing constructive things like these kits is more therapeutic for my PTSD than any medication … many veterans have a hard time with their leather kits, so I will help work the sewing for them."[10]

Art and craft programs for the disabled population now exist around the world, many with their own display space and gallery. One example is Spindleworks in Brunswick, Maine, in the northeast US. Spindleworks is an artistic collective of over forty artists working in multiple media, among them "weaving and other fiber and fabric arts."[11] The organization functions as a non-profit art center with a mission to help adults and children with disabilities live inclusive lives within Brunswick and surrounding areas. Art is exhibited continuously in the gallery and in other venues. The artists receive 75 percent of the sale price of their work that is sold through the gallery and volunteer in the space. Artists in the Spindleworks program receive studio space, supplies and guidance, as well as the therapeutic benefits of working in community with other artists. A quote on the Spindleworks' website by Rita Langlois reflects the benefits of the program: "Handicap, I heard about it but I ain't got it now." Fig. 7.19 shows the work of one of the weavers at the studio, Earl Black, whose profile in part reads: "As he will tell you, he dreams the colors at night and then comes and weaves those colors the next day. Earl could take apart and put together a four harness floor loom with his eyes closed."[12]

On the commercial side, a recent article in Specialty Fabrics Review (Eamon 2020) highlights the National Industries for the Blind, which was founded in 1938 and is the largest employer of blind people in the US (6,000 in 2019 including 600 veterans).[13] The organization helps secure manufacturing opportunities through a network of about one hundred nonprofit agencies producing products from mattresses to medical supplies. The organization, which has its headquarters in Alexandria VA, produces more than 7,000 different products under the SKILCRAFT® brand. The cut and sew divisions supply all branches of the US military and federal government with sewn products from pillowcases to apparel. Products range from the simple to the

Figure 7.19 *Earl Black with one of his weavings. Photo Credit: Spindleworks of Independence Association*

complex, such as flame-resistant fuel handler coveralls, which take 340 operational steps to complete. The company modifies equipment to fit individual needs, such as providing alignment guides, which allow for adaptive sewing. They also provide rehabilitation engineers as partners to help them convert labor from sighted to blind and to train the operators. National Industries for the Blind provides education to agencies about hiring employees who are blind and visually impaired, resources for instruction, grants and other resources such as accessible technology training. During the coronavirus pandemic, many of the agencies pivoted successfully to producing personal protective equipment (PPE) manufacturing and provided thousands of facemasks across the US.

The disabled community has long lived by the mantra "Nothing About Us Without Us," meaning that product design, services, policy, and other initiatives for their community cannot exist without disabled people having a seat at the table, or at least a person in the room.[14] This is as critical for the fashion industry as any other industry as it grapples with inclusion. Following that concept, today's fashion design industry now includes a number of disabled designers in its ranks. Carol Taylor is a quadriplegic designer who lives in Australia and in 2022 showed an adaptive collection at Afterpay Australia Fashion Week. The collection was co-created with the brand Christina Stephens, for which Carol is now a partner and lead designer. Taylor has spent much time as her own muse, working with different ways of fastening, placement of seams, fabrication choices, and other variations that can only be addressed through lived experience, direct or indirect. The partnership of Taylor with an existing adaptive brand brings that lived experience to the company.

Billy Price is co-founder of the brand BILLY Footwear, which has a design focus on shoes with universal principles built in. Billy Price broke his neck in a fall in 1996, subsequently becoming paralyzed from the waist down, and losing his ability to use his fingers. He founded the company after feeling that the adaptive market was lacking shoes that could be put on independently and were stylish at the same time. The core functionality, which occurs in multiple styles of BILLY Footwear shoe collections for women, men and children, is a zipper that curves from the top of shoe down around the front of the shoe and to the other side. This zipper opening allows the entire shoe to be opened up so that a foot can be placed into it rather than the foot having to adapt to enter into the shoe. Fig. 7.20a shows the Women's Rose Gold Billy Sneaker Lace mid-tops from the side, and then from the top (Fig. 7.20b) showing how they open up. Billy's story can be seen in a video on his website.[15]

Louise Linderoth is a Swedish fashion designer with her own eponymous line. She works primarily in denim, distressing and upcycling denim garments into sophisticated and avant-garde creations that are photographed on wheelchair models, but also fashion forward silhouettes for the abled community. Linderoth combines inclusive design with sustainable design.

Victoria Jenkins, founder of Unhidden, a UK-based brand, became disabled in her twenties and decided to start a company after encountering other

Figure 7.20a *Women's Rose Gold Billy Sneaker Lace mid-tops from the side. Photo by BILLY Footwear, billyfootwear.com*

Figure 7.20b *Women's Rose Gold Billy Sneaker Lace mid-tops from above, showing how they open up. Photo by BILLY Footwear, billyfootwear.com*

women's difficulties with clothing during a hospital stay. Unhidden embraces all aspects of sustainability—from the people who it serves as customers, to its entire supply chain. Transparency is evident on the company website, where a price breakdown is given for products. All models are indicated as volunteers.

The creativity of fashion models make fashion come to life, so it would be remiss not to mention their contributions here. The first person to go down a fashion runway in a wheelchair at New York Fashion Week was Danielle Sheypuk in 2014, modeling for Carrie Hammer. Danielle is a clinical psychologist based in New York and has used a wheelchair since the age of two. The first male disabled model to walk in NYC Fashion Week was the British model Jack Eyers, who wears a prosthetic leg after an amputation at the age of sixteen. He was also crowned Mr England 2017, the first amputee to gain that title. Jillian Mercado has become emblematic of wheelchair models since appearing in the Diesel "We Are Connected" campaign in 2014. Mercado attended FIT (Fashion Institute of Technology) in New York City, and has a degree in fashion merchandising management. Jillian is represented by IMG Models. Madeline Stuart is an Australian model born with Down's syndrome, who has walked runways in multiple global fashion weeks. She began her career with a viral Facebook posting and subsequent contact with companies, which has enabled her activism. Madeline is the first professional adult model with Down's syndrome, and the first person with Down's syndrome to be featured in *Vogue*. Aimee Mullins, whose photo was first presented in ch. 1 of this book, is one of the most notable, recognizable and legendary disabled models to have walked a fashion runway. She opened the late Alexander McQueen's runway show in 1999 and remained one of McQueen's muses until his death in 2010. Aimee has been photographed in multiple magazines in fashion, beauty and other media campaigns. She is a double amputee, having both of her legs amputated below the knee due to fibular hemimelia, and is a world-class athlete and actress.

Recently, organizations have been instrumental in providing impetus for fashion companies to include disabled models in their campaigns. These include the TV show, Britain's Missing Top Model, and Models of Diversity, founded by Angel Sinclair, a UK-based organization promoting equality, diversity and inclusion in fashion, beauty, and media. Models of Diversity promotes ethnicity, age, sizes above and below the industry "norm," disabilities and gender fluidity, and represent many professional models worldwide. Organizations such as this are contributing to the change needed in how the industry views its own products and services.

Summary

These stories, and many others like them, are evidence that disabled people are capable of contributing to all components of the fashion system. It is unknown at this time how many disabled designers are working for brands that are both household names and lesser known. The material selected for this chapter is just the tip of the iceberg but hopefully an introduction to the ways in which disabled makers and creators contribute.

To recap and make sense of this conversation, we have seen in Sarah Biffin how an artist with a disability not only used fashion to provide a visual cue as to the nature of her work but also how it was one of the conduits through which she was able to work. We have seen a military figure in Lord Nelson being active and inventive with a way to help protect his damaged eyesight. In the twentieth century we have seen individual designers meld the boundaries between disability and fashion by starting and maintaining successful businesses and organizations, and how designers like Billy Price are continuing that strong tradition today with a goal to helping all people universally, not just a few with special needs.

We have also seen how the group or collective has creative and commercial power. From Ernest Thesiger's Disabled Soldiers' Embroidery Industry to Annie Bindon Carter's Painted Fabrics, to the National Institute for the Blind, it can be observed that organizations which begin as therapeutic entities with community bonding and rehabilitation as the metric of success, can also be business minded, commercially successful and impactful while maintaining a collective spirit of collaboration and self-actualization.

I hope the chapter has provoked some opportunities for further discussion about how disabled people have been producing, inventing and selling commercially in the fashion ecosystem for a long time—maybe longer than they have been recognized by the industry as consumers.

Notes

1 McBrinn, J. (2015–16), "Nothing is more terrifying to me than to see Ernest Thesiger sitting under the lamplight doing this embroidery": Ernest Thesiger (1879–1961), "Expert Embroiderer", *For the Study of Textile Art, Design and History*, 43, 20–6.

2 McBrinn, J. (2016), "'The Work of Masculine Fingers': The Disabled Soldiers' Embroidery Industry, 1918–1955", *Journal of Design History*, 31 (1): 1–23.

3 McBrinn, J. (2019), "Refashioning Disability: The case of Painted Fabrics Ltd., 1915–1959", pp. 291–303, in P. Sparke and F. Fisher, (eds), *The Routledge Companion to Design Studies*, London and New York: Routledge Taylor & Francis Group.

4 Email communication, 2021

5 BBC Sheffield and South Yorkshire, (2014), The story of Painted Fabrics Ltd. Available online: http://www.bbc.co.uk/southyorkshire/content/articles/2008/11/03/painted_fabrics_limited_feature.shtml (accessed December 28, 2022).

6 Ibid.

7 McBrinn, J. (2016), "Refashioning Disability: The case of Painted Fabrics Ltd., 1915–1959", pp. 291–303, in P. Sparke and F. Fisher, (eds), *The Routledge Companion to Design Studies*, London and New York: Routledge Taylor & Francis Group.

8 Sheffield City Council, (2015), Painted Fabrics Ltd 1915–1959. Available online: https://www.sheffield.gov.uk/sites/default/files/docs/libraries-and-archives/archives-and-local-studies/research/Painted%20Fabrics%20Study%20Guide%20v1-1.pdf (accessed December 28, 2022).

9 Help Heal Veterans (2022), *Therapeutic Craft Kits*. Available online: https://healvets.org/ (accessed May 27, 2022).

10 Ibid.

11 Spindleworks Independence Association, (2022), *About*. Available online: https://spindleworks.independenceassociation.org/about (accessed November 15, 2022).

12 Spindleworks Independence Association, (2022), *Earl Black*. Available online: https://spindleworks.independenceassociation.org/artists#/earl-black (accessed December 28, 2022).

13 Eamon, H. (2020), "Breaking Barriers", *Specialty Fabrics Review*, November 2020: 43–5.

14 Charlton, J.I. (1998), *Nothing About Us Without Us: Disability Oppression and Empowerment*, Oakland, CA: University of California Press.

15 Billyfootwear.com (2022), *What's the Story?* Available online: https://billyfootwear.com/pages/about-us (accessed December 28, 2022).

8

Tying it all Together

Introduction

This final chapter will summarize the information shared in the other chapters of the book, analysing patterns of success as well as opportunities for progress. Key takeaways from the research are presented, including the following points:

- Despite the forward motion towards inclusivity in recent years, the fashion world still has huge potential and opportunities in this area

- Adaptation is not a new practice—it has been a necessary part of the world of disabled people for centuries, and is built intuitively into many non-Western items of dress. Does the process of adaptation still need to be included in discussions surrounding naming and branding fashion for disabled consumers? Can we look beyond the insufficiency of what has been designed in the past and find new methods of communicating—indeed, are new descriptors even needed?

- The intersection of fashion and disability is an example of how adaptation and necessity lead to innovation and creativity

- Fashion itself has been responsible for some disabling conditions

- Fashion must collaborate with other disciplines in order to survive and thrive

- The narrative is about makers as well as consumers; in the creative world, personal experience and connectivity is motivating and a key ingredient for success
- Role models and spokespeople have been and will continue to be important
- The academy has a huge part to play in the teaching of future professionals, in research and in community engagement
- Access to fashion and freedom of expression are civil rights.

8.1 Patterns of Success

It is my hope that in putting together the research for this book, I have been able to introduce some examples of how disability and fashion have intersected in a variety of ways throughout history. As a teacher and student of the historical developments behind fashion, in the researching and writing of this book I have developed a much richer understanding of the stories of people who have been "othered" by fashionable society, yet who have wanted to participate in the both the global movement we call Fashion and the act of self-fashioning as a form of appearance management and self-expression.

Contextual understanding is essential to making sense of why things are the way they are in any field of study. The question remains—although many "sparks" have been ignited over the years due to collaboration, government intervention, entrepreneurial ingenuity, academic research and outreach, and individual activism, are we at a point in the global fashion industry where we can use the word *integration* for the disabled community? There has certainly been an acceleration of progressive movement over the past ten years or so, and I am hopeful that this will continue to accelerate until we see inclusivity as the norm, not as a marketing add-on.

At this point, it might be helpful to look back at some of the key findings that have emerged from the historical evidence that has been pulled together in this work, in order that the sparks continue to evolve and become bigger fires that bring about permanent change and engagement.

1. Prior to the Start of the Ready-to-Wear Industry in the Nineteenth Century, Most Clothing was "Adapted" to Fit an Individual Body

If a person could afford a dressmaker or tailor, a desired garment was made to fit the body that you lived in. Variations in body shape, size and physical ability did not discriminate between rich and poor, but the rich and fashionable were able to hire skilled workers to clothe their bodies, no matter their body's variation from the fashionable norm. Thus, "adapted clothing" is not a new term. It is centuries old, and simply took a back seat as the ready-to-wear industry embraced a capitalist business model of standardization and mass-production for maximum profit. Even though fashion became more available to more people as a result of mass-production, the ready-to-wear industry also took away the possibility of engineering fabric around the body in a customized way. Prior to this gradual change, the majority of people who were not rich enough to hire a skilled seamstress or tailor were still skilled in home sewing by hand, but these skills declined in importance throughout the twentieth century as social, cultural, and gender roles changed in Western society. Although little is known about how people who could not afford tailors and dressmakers throughout history handled the making of clothing for their family members with a disability, it can be assumed that creative and user-focused adaptations and improvisations were carried out dependent upon the circumstances.

2. Many Non-Western Cultural Clothing Styles are Inherently Adaptive

The geometric shapes of traditional garments worn by non-Westerners allow for both personal and culturally prescribed draping and fastening to occur, thus freeing the body to shape the fabric, rather than the other way round (this concept of making the product do the work instead of the body is apparent in BILLY Footwear, mentioned in ch. 7). Some historians place the "beginning of [Western] fashion" in Late Medieval Europe, but this date simply marks the time when flat two-dimensional fabrics began to be cut and sewn into three-dimensional fitted garments using pattern pieces that conformed to the body.[1] Much non-Western, as well as Ancient fashion, relies on draping, pinning, belting, and other methods to wrap and fasten a piece of fabric around the body for warmth, protection, status, and expression. In doing so, this type of dressing liberates the body from Western fashionable architectural and structural norms, thus visibly equalizing bodies in an inclusive manner.

3. Disability has Contributed to Innovation and Entrepreneurship in the Fashion World

The disabled community has always relied on innovation and creativity to navigate an ableized world, in many cases just to survive. Some styles of clothing that were developed out of necessity have become part of the fashion lexicon, such as the Raglan sleeve, or today's Nike FlyEase shoes. If we expand this thinking to assistive devices, we can use the example of eyeglasses becoming an essential part of most luxury brands' portfolios, and prosthetics becoming fine art pieces.[2] These examples demonstrate the ways that crisis and need give rise to innovation, opportunity and mainstream adoption. Disability has given fashion an opportunity to advance into areas such as body part creation and artistic manipulation of the body beyond what we have imagined, at the same time giving assistive devices the opportunity to combine aesthetics and self-expression with functionality and end-use requirements.

4. Being Fashionable has in Itself been Disabling in Specific Historical Periods

This is most likely a controversial statement, but at certain times in history, being viewed as disabled *has* been the fashionable norm. For fashionable women, who were still considered the property of men well into the nineteenth century and second class citizens well into the twentieth, subjugation in the form of clothing such as corsets and heavy undergarments rendered them disabled in that their clothing restricted them physically, echoing the cultural restrictions placed on them by fashionable society.

5. Fashion has and Should Continue to Play an Important Role in Rehabilitation and Therapy

We have witnessed how collaboration across disciplines leads to progressive ideas and practical outcomes. How likely is it that Helen Cookman would have founded Functional Fashions without Dr. Howard Rusk asking for her help on an apparently overlooked aspect of his patients' rehabilitation efforts at New York University Medical Center's Institute of Physical and Rehabilitation Medicine? Current designers working in adaptive fashion stress the importance of fashion designers working with and understanding the role of professionals in the fields of healthcare, therapy, and biomechanics. Open Style Lab is a contemporary example of this philosophy in action.

6. Disabled Makers have an Important Place in Fashion

This book presented evidence that disabled people have been involved with the making of consumer goods for many years, but it was not until the late nineteenth century that organizations intentionally advocated for these workers (the London flower makers) and then introduced therapeutic outcomes for them when the amount of visibly disabled people began to increase (Painted Fabrics Inc., The Disabled Soldiers' Embroidery Industry). Making things with textiles might have begun as a way to re-introduce disabled people into the workforce, but thoughtful and well-managed work with embroidery, printing, and other textile arts showed that benefits extended and added value for the maker and consumer. Organizations that began purely as therapeutic and philanthropic turned into businesses that created and sold unique pieces of artwork, and in the case of Painted Fabrics, may have contributed to a brand-new artform, according to the opinion of contemporary art professionals. In addition, some of these organizations have become models for how today's disabled population can be engaged in the workforce and live a self-actualized life in an adapted environment.

7. People's Motivation for Inclusivity in Fashion Stems Largely from Personal Involvement but True Inclusivity Must Involve a Change in the Profile of the Industry

Many designers who have been mentioned in this book—from the 1950s and 1960s to the present day—have had personal engagement with disability. Helen Cookman, Mrs. Van Davis Odell, Lucy Jones, Grace Jun, Justin LeBlanc, Tommy Hilfiger have all built upon their personal experiences and used their skills to advance the field and produce change. In moving "adaptive fashion" towards the mainstream, personal experience can be substituted by empathetic and hands-on immersion in the life of the user of a designed product. Designers must take it upon themselves to find these immersive points of contact, whether through training and/or continual connections with communities of lived experience. However, the true voice of the consumer resides in the inclusion of the disabled designer/maker taking a seat at the table and true inclusivity can only begin when companies start to "look like" their customer base.

8. Role Models and Icons are Important Champions for Inclusivity

Just as Instagram has its share of celebrities pushing fashions forward through endorsements and influencing the way we adapt our personal styles, the disabled community has experienced role models who have shown how to co-exist with abelized fashion. Frida Kahlo, most often lauded for her contributions to twentieth-century fine art, generated just as much interest and celebrity attention from the way she styled and displayed her body, using customized and adapted clothing pieces themselves borrowed from indigenous culture. Frida made full use of the medium of photography to get her artistic and expressive viewpoint across. P.T. Barnum's "staging" of Lavinia Warren and her husband Charles Stratton (aka "General" Tom Thumb), although a created facade in many respects, certainly propelled little people into the fashion limelight and engaged important contemporary fashion houses with disability, perhaps for the first time in such a public way. Adaptive fashion would not be where it is today without the efforts of models like Jillian Mercado and design activists like Sinéad Burke, whose writings and speeches have galvanized awareness and action.

9. Some Brands have been Building Accommodations into Clothing for Years

By beginning the design process with a philosophy of accommodation, the Florence Eiseman brand of high-end children's clothing, which opened in the United States in 1945, produced items of clothing that already allowed for physical accommodation. The company incorporated universal design principles by eliminating constricting waistlines; featuring the "add-a-growth" hem; widening pants to accommodate leg-braces; reinforcing underarm seams; cutting dresses longer for wheelchair use, plus countless other details. In addition, the brand promoted "self-help," thus instilling confidence and self-esteem. By employing advertising campaigns showing the same item of clothing on an abled child next to a disabled child, Eiseman is an example of inclusivity and equality in the US fashion industry that has existed for decades.

10. Academic and Industry Collaboration is Key

In doing the research for this book and the years of experience of working in this area, perhaps the most frustrating point is to be aware of the years of good work and research that has been carried out in higher education, but also knowing that much of it has not made its way into the mainstream fashion lexicon. If customers don't know about the product or how to access it, the research effort is for nothing. If customers don't know, then they cannot demand and therefore there is no "pull" through the fashion industry. Collaboration between educators and brands is the means by which this can be improved.

Academic curricula must be better designed to include training for fashion students in the design, production and marketing for products targeted towards people with disabilities and this training must be integrated from the moment a student sets foot into a classroom. If a tailor's training book from the eighteenth century can devote pages to patternmaking and construction guidelines on how to fit an asymmetrical or "differently-shaped" body, then our modern textbooks should be written to include these same concepts.

11. Fashion is a Civil Rights Movement

In most parts of the world, we have rights granted to us as citizens of a country. If those rights include the freedom to self-actualize and to enjoy equality with other citizens, then fashion, with its ability to communicate our personal style and values in a non-verbal way, is a tool for communicating and celebrating those rights. We should all have the ability to fashion our bodies in a way that provides comfort, protection and freedom of self-expression, but if that fashion is inaccessible, then our rights are being curtailed. Fashion can also be a tool for civil rights. What better way to proclaim our commitment to a cause than to wear it on our bodies?

12. The Tools for Good Design are Already in Place

If we peek back into history one more time, many of the progressive steps forward have been a result of simple ideas executed with simple tools. Contemporary times offer a multitude of advanced technologies, but they are for nought if limited primarily to the abled population by access and cost. Throughout the history of design, many of the significant points of progress with technology for disabled people have eventually become used and mainstreamed by the abled. The trickle-down effect is apparent in the Universal Design movement, where items such as door levers used in place of door knobs became universal simply because they were easier for *everyone* to use. A technology that assists someone to more easily don and doff their clothing will most likely be well received by everyone (see the Nike FlyEase shoe as an example, and the widespread use of Velcro fastening tape across multiple consumer groups). At the same time, the most significant advance in fastening systems in recent years has been magnets, a centuries-old technology. Fashion can utilize these tried and tested tools, but perhaps there is also room for improvement and new tools, especially for donning and doffing of products.

13. There is no Disabled Fashion, there is Only Fashion

Fashion should exist for all, not just for a few. A change in "ability" should not prevent someone from having access to nice things. At the time of writing, changes in the way we approach gender are impacting the fashion world, resulting in a thoughtful approach towards gender-neutral fashions in the retail market. Can the fashion industry adopt the same approach and become ability-neutral moving forward?

8.2 Tying it All Together

Where we're at right now is a very positive place. In the three or so years spent researching this book, I have witnessed seismic changes in the amount and type of (a) fashion available to the disabled community, (b) coverage in the press and (c) models on runways across the world, from New York Fashion Week to small academic programs' student shows. Social media has had a lot to do with these changes, but there is also a generational shift commanding and steering this change. Generation Z is smart, aware, empathetic and not about to allow their fashion industry to move forward leaving anyone behind. Television and the movie industry is also starting to understand the importance of inclusivity and of normalizing disability in its product offerings. The winner of the Outstanding Performance category at the Screen Actors Guild and the Best Picture at the Oscars in 2022 was the movie *CODA*, the first movie about deaf people starring deaf people, with the deaf actor Troy Kotsur taking the SAG and the Oscar awards for Best Supporting Actor. The art world is creating content such as the Raw Beauty Project, an art platform celebrating women and artists with disabilities through photography and other 2D art forms, telling stories and giving voice through art to the thirty-six million women in the US with disabilities.

The changes that are currently happening in art and culture are also allowing more people to participate in the fashion world as a means of self-expression, even if the demographic group to which they belong has been historically excluded from the industry. Julia Twigg, in her examination of the interaction between fashion and age explains how:

> Fashion is for many a source of joy and uplift. There is aesthetic pleasure to be derived from colour and textile, from the feel and look of dress. It can be positive and life-enhancing, as much as oppressive and objectifying. Dress also has a significant part to play in the process of being visible of occupying social and cultural space in a confident manner . . . dress, especially if chosen and worn in a confident and positive manner, can be part of an assertion of value, a repudiation of invisibility.
>
> TWIGG 2013: 4[3]

At the same time, there is always room for improvement. Sometimes efforts come off as patronizing and sympathetic, instead of normalizing and empowering. The message that disability is a state that can be cured or healed, rather than a continuum that affects all of humanity (we are all going to get old at some point and many of us have been temporarily disabled in our lives), is still somewhat prevalent. Some brand messaging continues to focus on inspiration rather than normalization. Even though this book does not try to explore the retail distribution interaction between fashion and disability, the intertwining of brands' new adaptive lines with existing products should extend to the retail environment. It is still extremely challenging to navigate a brick-and-mortar store from a wheelchair. Tables are piled high with product, sometimes out of reach from both a height and depth perspective. Back walls are loaded with merchandise two or three times the height of a person in a wheelchair or using crutches. The recent downsizing and loss of employees due to the pandemic has severely affected the ability to find assistance in a store when needed. We are still not at the point where retail dressing rooms are accessible despite the ADA; in fact, most are in distant corners and at the very back of large department and discount stores. I would go so far as to challenge the lengths to which retailers are prepared to go in order to associate themselves with disabled people. Julia Twigg talks about a "moving younger" phenomenon that exists in the fashion industry. (Twigg 2013: 148) Can we call some of these branding and distribution challenges "moving abled"? When goods designed for an aging population are displayed on youthful models, we call it ageism. When it happens with disability, let's call it ableism.

8.3 Where we could be Heading

Now that you know that fashion and disability have intersected for a fairly lengthy period of time, it might be slightly easier to imagine what future discourse could look like. The fashion industry is waking up to the fact that disabled consumers have buying power and they are not afraid to use it.[4] Twenty years ago the "market-of-one" mentality, which was the industry response to my initial work, is changing to embrace the broad group of "adaptive" and savvy consumers who are demanding action and accessibility to fashion brands.[5] Of course the road needs to continue to be activist. It's important to continue the discussion, with our wallets, our online network and our continual promotion of products and services that are inclusive. Those of us in the abled community can do more to engage with disability and become comfortable with it. As I've mentioned before, we will all get old and less-abled one day. If you have ever had an arm in a sling, or a leg in a brace, you have been temporarily disabled. Think for a minute about how this impacted your ability to don, wear and doff your favorite clothes and accessories. Next time you're in a store, sit in a chair and look at the displays and racks, noting how many are out of reach, even to look at a price tag or informational label.

I'm hoping there is room for many more books such as this one. Many of these stories are just tips of the iceberg, with a wealth of information waiting to be researched. There is more left out than went into this volume, and much, much more primary evidence to be uncovered in museums, archives, and libraries. The history of disability fashion is deserving of a deeper dive and continued exploration. Many groups have been omitted from the historical stories we are learning from—yet there is so much to learn.

The academic world has potentially great power to change this narrative. Students of fashion can demand that courses be offered in all aspects of inclusivity in fashion, from design to merchandising and marketing. Institutions teaching fashion can engage with disabled fit models, consultants, and organizations, and promote the opportunity for faculty, staff, and students to engage with disabled people who are happy to share their needs and explain systems that work for them. Fashion design trainees can keep a keen eye out for new developments and practise what is read and seen. In fashion competitions and shows which have a public-facing component let's always submit adaptive fashions within a line. Faculty members and administrators should incorporate relevant content into classes, carrying out research that truly engages with the disabled community, and publish books and articles to stay on the cutting edge of new developments. It is also most important to bring students along to conferences and meetings with industry and other researchers in the field. Additionally, adhere to the person in the room practice and hire disabled faculty and teaching assistants. Finally on this subject, let's look around the classroom and ask ourselves how inviting our environment is for disabled students. Are we even educating disabled students?

Bringing this chapter and book to a close requires that I return to the beginning of ch. 1 and reiterate that this is primarily a story about fashion, a phenomenon that enables every human body to be able to self-fashion, or create their appearance, as a form of self-expression. Leaving people out of the mix is unacceptable if we are to progress as a civil society. We have come to understand that exclusionary practices are not beneficial. In writing this book I have been reminded once again that history offers hope, guidance and humility to situations if we are open to learn from its lessons. I hope that you have found something important to you in this book and will be inspired to think more about its meaning and to do what you can with the resources and energy that you have at your disposal.

8.4 Disability Fashion History Timeline

Date	Event	Chapter/Section
1585	*The Works of Ambroise Paré*, showing the invention of an iron corset developed to "straighten" bodies, is published	2.2
1660	Mun Verney's "suits" of doublet and breeches are adapted for his disability	2.2
1702	King William III's sleeved waistcoat is adapted after a fall from his horse results in a broken collarbone	2.2

1720–30	Platt Hall sleeved waistcoat is adapted to fit a man with suggested diagnosis of scoliosis	2.2
1754	William Hay publishes *Deformity: An Essay*	2.3
1797–1820	Englishmen of Fashion, Admiral Lord Horatio Nelson and King George III have clothing adapted for their disabilities	3.1
1840s	Tailoring books, authored by G. Walker and J. Couts, are published, containing pattern adaptation instructions for practitioners	3.1
1850	Raglan sleeve developed by Aquascutum of London as an adaptation for the military leader's disability	3.1
1860s	Lavinia Warren (Mrs. Tom Thumb) emerges as a fashion leader	3 Boxed Profile
Late 1800s	Prosthetic production ramps up in the United States after the Civil War concludes in 1865	3.2
c.1903	Queen Alexandra's gown is adapted for body asymmetry	3.2
1915	Painted Fabrics Inc. begins as a volunteer effort led by Annie Bindon Carter	7.1
1918	Disabled Soldiers' Embroidery Industry begins as a volunteer effort led by Ernest Thesiger	7.1
1930s and 1940s	Frida Kahlo emerges as an advocate for fashion and disability through her artistic self-expression	4 Boxed Profile
Mid-1940s	"National Employ the Physically Handicapped Week" signed into existence by President Truman; Woodrow Wilson Rehabilitation Center opens in Virginia	4.1
1952	Howard Rusk engages a fashion designer, Helen Cookman, to design clothing for New York University Medical Center Rehabilitation Institute	4.3
1955	Eleanor Boettke began her research into clothing for disabled women at the University of Connecticut	4.2
1961	*Clothes for the Physically Handicapped Homemaker,* written by Clarice Scott, is published by the Agricultural Research Service, part of the USDA	4.2
Late 1950s–1973	The Functional Fashions label engages known designers in the creation of fashion for disabled consumers	4.3, 4.4

Date	Event	Chapter/Section
Mid-1960s	Other efforts ramp up in the US, including Help the Handicapped, VGRS, Fashion-Able, Leinenweber's and JC Penney	4.4
Late 1960s	Joan Lord begins pioneering work at the Shirley Institute, United Kingdom; Disabled Living Foundation, also based in the UK, assembles a Clothing Advisory Panel	4.5
1973	US Rehabilitation Act is passed, marking the first significant broad-based legislation for disabled Civil Rights	5.1
1977	Fashion Design Research studio is started by M. Dolores Quinn at Drexel University, Philadelphia	5.2
1979	*Clothing for the Handicapped, the Aged, and Other People with Special Needs*, written by Adeline M. Hoffman, is published	5.1
1984	*Clothing: The Portable Environment*, written by Susan M. Watkins, is published	6.4
1989	Center for Accessible Housing, now the Center for Universal Design, is established at North Carolina State University	5.2
1990	Americans with Disabilities Act is passed; Simplicity's *Design without Limits* book, written by M. Dolores Quinn and Renee Weiss Chase, is published	6.1; 5.2
1992	Lamb and Kallal's FEA Consumer Needs Model is published	6.4
1995	Disability Discrimination Act is passed in the United Kingdom	6.1
2010–2020	Mainstream retailers Zappos, Target, Hilfiger Adaptive, and Nike begin to offer adaptive products as part of their product mix	6.2
2014	New York Fashion Week shows a collection with the first disabled model	7.2

Notes

1   For a full discussion on "The Birth of Fashion", see Chapter Eight of Linda Welters and Abby Lillethun's book, *Fashion History, A Global View*, (2018), published by Bloomsbury Academic.

2   For a comprehensive discussion on this topic, see Pullin, G. (2009), *Design meets disability*, Cambridge, MA: MIT Press

3   Twigg, J. (2013), *Fashion and Age: Dress, the Body and Later Life,* London, UK: Bloomsbury Academic.

4   *DiverseAbility Magazine* cites an American Institute for Research study listing the total disposable income for U.S. adults with disabilities at about $490 billion.

5   Carroll, K.E. (2002), *"Innovations and Improvisations: A study in specialized product development focused on business clothing for women with physical disabilities",* unpublished doctoral dissertation, Virginia Tech, Blacksburg VA.

Appendix A: Resources

The Barnum Museum, Bridgeport, USA
www.barnum-museum.org

Bucks Museum (Buckinghamshire County Museum), Aylesbury, UK
National Collection of the Embroiders Guild and Disabled Soldiers' Embroidery Industry
    artifacts
https://www.discoverbucksmuseum.org/partners/the-embroiderer-guild/

Claydon House, Buckinghamshire, UK
National Trust property, home of Mun Verney's adapted clothing
https://www.nationaltrust.org.uk/visit/oxfordshire-buckinghamshire-berkshire/claydon

The Commercial pattern archive
https://copa.apps.uri.edu/index.php

Costume Institute, Metropolitan Museum of Art, New York City, USA
https://www.metmuseum.org/about-the-met/collection-areas/the-costume-institute

Cooper Hewitt, Smithsonian Design Museum, New York, USA
Access+Ability exhibit, December 15, 2017 to September 3, 2018
https://www.cooperhewitt.org/channel/access-ability/

Kent State University Museum, Kent, USA
(dis)ABLEDBEAUTY: The evolution of beauty, disability, and ability exhibit, July 2016 to
    March 2017
https://oaks.kent.edu/ksumuseum/3

Milwaukee Art Museum, Milwaukee, USA (in collaboration with Chipstone Foundation)
Functional Fashions Installation, March 23, 2019 to April 1, 2020
https://chipstone.org/content.php/27/Current-Exhibitions

Painted Fabrics Project Group
paintedfabricssheffield@gmail.com

Platt Hall/Manchester Art Gallery, Manchester, UK
Home of eighteenth-century adapted embroidered waistcoat
www.manchestergalleries.org

Royal Ontario Museum, Toronto, Canada
Fashion follows Form: Designs for Sitting exhibit, June 21, 2014 to January 25, 2015

https://www.rom.on.ca/en/exhibitions-galleries/exhibitions/fashion-follows-form-designs-for-sitting

Sheffield City Archives, Sheffield, UK
Home to Painted Fabrics archived material
www.sheffield.gov.uk/archives

Smithsonian Museum, National Museum of American History, Washington DC, USA
Special Olympics at 50, online exhibit
https://americanhistory.si.edu/exhibitions/special-olympics-50

The University of Alberta, Anne Lambert Clothing and Textiles Collection, Edmonton, Canada
Misfits: Bodies, Dress, and Sustainability, April 12, 2017 to September 13, 2017
https://clothingtextiles.ualberta.ca/2018/06/07/misfits-bodies-dress-and-sustainability/

The Victoria and Albert Museum, London, UK
Frida Kahlo: Making Her Self Up exhibit, June 16, 2018 to November 18, 2018
https://www.vam.ac.uk/exhibitions/frida-kahlo-making-her-self-up

Weston Park Museum, Sheffield, UK
Home to several Painted Fabrics artifacts
https://www.sheffieldmuseums.org.uk/visit-us/weston-park-museum/

Museum of Wisconsin Art, West Bend, USA
Florence Eiseman: Designing Childhood for the American Century, June 11, 2017 to October 8, 2017
https://wisconsinart.org/exhibitions/florence-eiseman/

Index

The letter *f* following an entry indicates a page with a figure.